THEORIES *and* METHODS

Morag MacDonald
Lee Harvey,
and Jane Hill

Series Editor: Paul Selfe

Hodder & Stoughton

DDER HEADLINE GROUP

DEDICATION

In memory of my father, J. Arthur Corby.
For my mother, Mona Corby.

Orders: please contact Bookpoint Ltd, 39 Milton Park, Abingdon, Oxon OX14 4TD.
Telephone: (44) 01235 400414, Fax: (44) 01235 400454. Lines are open from 9.00–6.00,
Monday to Saturday, with a 24 hour message answering service.
Email address: orders@bookpoint.co.uk

A catalogue record for this title is available from The British Library

ISBN 0 340 73738 7

First published 2000
Impression number 10 9 8 7 6 5 4 3 2
Year   2005 2004 2003 2002 2001 2000

Copyright © 2000, Lee Harvey, Morag MacDonald and Jane Hill

Cover painting by Pablo Picasso: 'Head and Guitar', 1927. © Succession Picasso / DACS 1999

Typeset by Transet Limited, Coventry, England.
Printed in Great Britain for Hodder & Stoughton Educational, a division of
Hodder Headline plc, 338 Euston Road, London NW1 3BH by Redwood Books,
Trowbridge, Wilts.

CONTENTS

ACHNOWLEDGEMENTS

The publishers would like to thank the Hulton Getty picture collection for permission to reproduce the photo on page 23, Emma Lee and Life File for the picture on page 64, Steve Eason and Photofusion for the picture on page 91 and the Ronald Grant Archive for the picture on page 103.

1

INTRODUCTION

HOW TO USE THE BOOK

EACH CHAPTER IN this book examines one or more of the central debates relating to sociological theories and methods and their application. The text is devised for readers with little or no background knowledge in the subject, and there are Study Points and Activities throughout to encourage a consideration of the issues raised. Student readers are advised to make use of these and answer them either on paper or in group discussion, a particularly fruitful way of learning; they will assist them to develop the skills of interpretation, analysis and evaluation. There are many ways of preparing for an exam, but a thorough understanding of the material is obviously crucial.

Each chapter is structured to give a clear understanding of the authors, concepts and issues that you need to know about. To assist understanding and facilitate later revision, it is often helpful to make concise notes.

MAKING NOTES FROM THE BOOK

Linear notes
- Bold headings establish key points: names, theories and concepts.
- Subheadings indicate details of relevant issues.
- A few numbered points list related arguments.

Diagram or pattern notes
- Use a large blank sheet of paper and write a key idea in the centre.
- Make links between this and related issues.
- Show also the connections between sub issues which share features in common.

Both systems have their advantages and disadvantages, and may take some time to perfect. Linear notes can be little more than a copy of what is already in the book and patterned notes can be confusing. But if you practise the skill, they can reduce material efficiently and concisely becoming invaluable for revision. Diagrammatic notes may be very useful for those with a strong visual memory and provide a clear overview of a whole issue, showing patterns of interconnection. The introduction of helpful drawings or a touch of humour into the format is often a good way to facilitate the recall of names, research studies and complex concepts.

Activity
Make a diagram to show the two ways of making notes with their possible advantages and disadvantages

SKILLS ADVICE

Students must develop and display certain skills for their examination and recognise which ones are being tested in a question. The clues are frequently in key words in the opening part. The skill domains are:

1 **Knowledge and understanding:** the ability to discuss the views of the main theorists; their similarities and differences; the strengths and weaknesses of evidence. To gain marks students must display this when asked to *explain, examine, suggest a method, outline reasons*.

2 **Interpretation, application and analysis:** the use of evidence in a logical, relevant way, either to show how it supports arguments or refutes them. Students must show this ability when asked *identify, use items A/B/C, draw conclusions from a table*.

3 **Evaluation:** the skill of assessing evidence in a balanced way so that logical conclusions follow. Students can recognise this skill when asked to *assess, critically examine, comment on levels of reliability, compare and contrast*, or if asked *to what extent*.

Activity
Draw an evaluation table, as below, using the whole of an A4 page. Examine studies as you proceed in your work and fill in the relevant details. Keep it for revision purposes.

Sociologist		
Title of the study	Strengths	Weaknesses
Verdict		
Judgement/justification		

REVISION ADVICE

- Keep clear notes at all times in a file or on disk (with back up copy).
- Be familiar with exam papers and their demands.
- Become familiar with key authors, their theories, their research and sociological concepts.

Activity

Make and keep **Key Concept Cards**, as shown below.

COLLECTIVE CONSCIENCE

Key idea

A term used by **Durkheim** meaning:

- The existence of a social and moral order exterior to individuals and acting upon them as an independent force.
- The shared sentiments, beliefs and values of individuals which make up the **collective conscience.**
- In **traditional societies** it forms the basis of social order.
- As societies modernise the collective conscience weakens: **mechanical solidarity** is replaced by **organic solidarity**.

Key theorist: Emile Durkheim

Syllabus area: Functionalism

EXAMINATION ADVICE

To develop an effective method of writing, answers should be:

- **Sociological:** use the language and research findings of sociologists; do not use anecdotal opinion gathered from people not involved in sociology to support arguments.
- **Adequate in length:** enough is written to obtain the marks available.

- **Interconnected** with other parts of the syllabus (such as stratification, gender, ethnicity).
- **Logical:** the answer follows from the relevant evidence.
- **Balanced:** arguments and counter arguments are weighed; references are suitable.
- **Accurate:** reliable data is obtained from many sources.

The three skill areas on page 2 should be demonstrated, so that the question is answered effectively.

In displaying knowledge, the student is not necessarily also demonstrating interpretation.

- This must be specified with phrases like 'Therefore, this study leads to the view that...'
- Sections of answers should hang together, one leading to the next. This shows how the question is being answered by a process of analysis based on the evidence.
- Reach a conclusion based on the evidence used and the interpretations made.

The skill of evaluation is often regarded (not necessarily accurately) as the most problematic. Evaluation means being judge and jury; the strengths and weaknesses of evidence is assessed and an overall judgement about its value is made. To evaluate an argument or theory, consider whether it usefully opens up debate; explains the events studied; does it have major weaknesses?

Activity
Look through some past examination papers and pick out the evaluation questions. Underline the evaluation words and work out which skills are required.

COURSEWORK ADVICE

Coursework provides an opportunity to carry out a study using primary and/or secondary data to investigate an issue of sociological interest, and must address theoretical issues. The suggestions included at the end of each chapter may be adapted or used to generate further ideas. Final decision must be agreed with a teacher or tutor.

MAKING A PLAN

Before starting a piece of coursework, you should make a plan:

1 Read and make notes from articles describing research projects in journals.

2 Have a clear aim in mind; choose an issue that interests you and is within your ability.
3 Decide more precisely what you want to know; establish a simple hypothesis to test.
4 Select a range of possible methods; consider both quantitative and qualitative.
5 Decide on a range of possible sources of information.
6 List the people to whom you can seek help, perhaps including a statistician.

WRITING THE PROJECT

1 Seek frequent advice from a teacher or tutor.
2 Check the weighting for different objectives in the marking scheme.
3 Keep clear notes throughout, including new ideas and any problems that arise.
4 Limit its length (maximum 5,000 words).
5 Label and index the study in the following way:
   a **Rationale:** a reason for choosing the subject; preliminary observations on the chosen area
   b **Context:** an outline of the theoretical and empirical context of the study
   c **Methodology:** a statement of the methodology used and reasons for selecting it
   d **Method:** state the methods used for collecting data
   e **Content:** presentation of the evidence and/or argument including results
   f **Evaluation:** the outcomes are weighed and strengths and weaknesses noted.
   g **Sources:** all the sources of information are listed.
OR
   a **Title**
   b **Contents**
   c **Abstract:** a brief summary of the aims, methods, findings and evaluation.
   d **Rationale**
   e **The Study**
   f **Research Diary**
   g **Bibliography**
   h **Appendix:** to include proposal for the study, single examples of a questionnaire or other data-gathering instrument and transcripts of interviews.
   i **Annex:** to include raw data gathered.

In this book quotations have been printed in italics. In your own work you should supply any quotes in **regular type, indented or within quotation marks**. Remember to supply the source of any quotes in your work.

Paul Selfe
Series editor

2

THINKING SOCIOLOGICALLY

Introduction

THIS CHAPTER OUTLINES the key processes of sociological practice. Thinking sociologically requires us to question our everyday assumptions about the world in which we live. We do this by developing theories, which we then compare with our experiences and observations of the world. Theorising about society requires that we actively seek out evidence to help us develop and substantiate our theories.

Table 2.1: *Key concepts and questions in this chapter*	
KEY CONCEPTS	KEY QUESTIONS
Theory	What is the purpose of theory? How do we develop theories? At what level do we theorise (society / micro)?
Epistemology	What is knowledge? How do we produce it?
Ontology	How do we define the subject matter of sociology?
Method	How do we collect evidence?
Methodology	Why do we adopt a particular aproach to sociology? What is the relationship between theory and method?
Data	What counts as evidence in sociology?
Fact	Can facts exist independently of theory?

Table continued on subsequent page

KEY CONCEPTS	KEY QUESTIONS

Table 2.1 *Key concepts and questions in this chapter* (continued)

KEY CONCEPTS	KEY QUESTIONS
Values	What do we mean by values? Can we distinguish between facts and values?
Empiricism	Can we know the world solely through sense experience?
Empirical	How does 'empirical' differ from 'empiricism'?
Positivism	Can we reproduce the natural scientific approach when studying the social world?
Phenomenology	Do people's meanings need to be taken into account when studying the social world?
Critical	How do historical, political and economic factors affect people's experiences of the social world?

THEORISING

Sociology is the study of society and if you want to understand society then it is important that you develop theories about how society works. It is possible to live in society without theorising about the way that it works, in the same way that it is possible to drive a car without understanding the mechanical and chemical processes that make the car move.

On the other hand, theorising is not something difficult or 'academic'. We do it in our ordinary lives. A theory is nothing more than a notion about why or how something is as it is. If we catch a cold we usually 'theorise' that it is because we have been in contact with someone else with a cold or because the weather has changed, or because we are 'run down'.

In sociology, a 'theory' is thus a notion about aspects of the social world. In essence, theories answer questions such as:

- Why do we have poverty?
- Why does racial prejudice exist and what purpose does it serve?
- How do some people become criminals?
- Why are women rarely in positions of power?
- How does 'the family' work and in what circumstances does it break down?

All of these are theoretical questions.

THEORISING ABOUT THE NATURE OF SOCIETY

Sociologists also ask theoretical questions of much wider issues than the examples given above. Sociology is the study of the relationship between society and the individuals that make up society. So, in order to study the social world, theoretical assumptions are made about the nature of society and the nature of the people within it. These assumptions are sometimes called *ontological* assumptions (ontology is a term that is used to describe the study of 'being'). In sociology ontological assumptions can be more simply described as the ways in which we choose to define our subject matter (Jones, 1993). For example, some sociologists assume that society is external to individuals. Thus, they choose to treat the people who make up society in exactly the same way as scientists treat the inanimate objects of their study.

THEORISING ABOUT HOW TO PRODUCE KNOWLEDGE

Sociologists need to make decisions about the most appropriate way to produce knowledge about the topics that they are studying. These decisions are sometimes called *epistemological* decisions, which is a rather grand way of talking about theories of knowledge. As we will see in more detail in Chapter 3, some early sociology assumed that there was only one way to produce knowledge (one epistemology); to adopt the same processes of knowledge production utilised by natural scientists. This research tradition is called *positivism* but, as we shall see, it is not the only research tradition.

LEVELS OF THEORISING

'Theory' is an all-encompassing term that covers a variety of levels of theorising:

- specific theories;
- general theories of social action;
- broader sociological research traditions.

A theory can be very specific, dealing with a limited aspect of sociology, such as a theory of deviant behaviour. For example, Howard Becker theorised that the ways in which people attach negative labels to others may lead to further deviant behaviour on the part of those so labelled; this is known as labelling theory.

A sociological theory can also be wider, attempting to cover all social activity. This is usually known as a sociological perspective. For example, in *functionalism* a stable society is seen to result from agreement about norms, that is, how we should behave. This perspective also assumes that there is agreement about what is important in a society. For example, the work of Émile Durkheim reveals a concern for social order. Durkheim thinks of society much as a human body in which all the separate parts, the heart, the lungs, the liver, and so on need to work well in order for an individual to be healthy. In the same way, a healthy society requires individuals to work together for the good of society as a whole. An alternative view, found in various conflict perspectives, challenges the idea that society is characterised by consensus. According to these conflict perspectives, society is characterised by various structural inequalities such as wealth, gender and 'race', which make consensus impossible.

At a third level, it is possible to theorise about what constitutes sociological knowledge. As we will see below, in the work of Durkheim, Marx and Weber, the different ways in which sociologists define their subject matter affect the ways in which they choose to produce knowledge about the social world. These are known as sociological research traditions.

METHOD

We have seen that it is necessary to develop some theories to begin to understand how society works. Equally, we need to develop *methods* to collect evidence to support or challenge theories. We could make up theories on the basis of what we think we already know but these would be conjectures that would be unlikely to convince anyone else. To develop convincing theories it is necessary to collect evidence and show how the theory relates to it or develops from it.

Method, in social science, refers to the tools used to collect data or evidence. The collection of data or evidence is necessary if our explanation, interpretation or understanding of the social world is to be based on more than theoretical speculation.

The key to social research is to obtain a balance between 'data' and 'theory'. Knowledge that is based entirely on observation or experiment is known as *empirical* knowledge. Similarly, knowledge based solely on theoretical analysis is *theoretical* knowledge. The goal of social research is to merge theoretical and empirical knowledge so that we can account for social phenomena in a way that connects our theories about the social world to observable experience of it.

Study point
Write down which types of evidence you think are appropriate for sociological enquiry. Devise a method by which you could find out whether the pastoral care system in the institution in which you are studying is working efficiently.

DATA AND EVIDENCE

We have referred to 'data' or 'evidence' and these are closely related terms. Data (the plural of 'datum') refers to things that are known or taken as given and usually provide the basis for making inferences. Evidence is a slightly broader term that refers to things that are used or allowed in support of a conclusion. Evidence may include indicators, signs, observations, statements, information given personally or drawn from documents. The two terms, data and evidence, are often used interchangeably in social science.

For example, if someone points out to you a tall person, with short hair, wearing a business suit, whose name is Terry and who works in an engineering firm you may infer from the data that the person is male. You would not always be correct. Indeed, you may consider the data insufficient to draw an inference. Looked at slightly differently, you may draw on the evidence as support for the conclusion that the person is male. On the other hand, you may regard the evidence as inconclusive.

At root, all data or evidence relies on 'observation'. In social science an 'observation' has a wider meaning than in common speech. Observation is not just restricted to the act of directly seeing something. An observation can include any of the senses. Furthermore, an observation can be second-hand and provided it is somehow recorded or transmitted, via print, conversation, tape or any other medium it counts as an observation.

So, in social science, evidence or data may take many different forms, including

- observations of actions;
- conversations;
- interviews;
- completed questionnaires;
- published documents;

- unpublished documents;
- official statistics;
- video recordings;
- reports and images in the mass media;
- 'cultural objects' such as paintings, films, plays.

EMPIRICAL AND EMPIRICISM

The term 'empirical data' is used widely in social science. In theory, this should only refer to observation or experiment that permits inferences. In practice the term 'empirical data' is used in social science to refer to any data or evidence. Hence, given our definition of data, there is no need, in practice, to preface it with the descriptor 'empirical'. Conversely, in practice, an 'empirical study' is one that draws on data or evidence in making inferences or conclusions.

However, one distinction that you need to be aware of is that between 'empirical' and 'empiricist' (Pawson, 1989). Empirical, as we have seen, means using data as part of the research. An empiricist approach is one that assumes that knowledge can be derived directly from observation and is opposed to theoretical conjecture. It is beyond the scope of this chapter to examine 'empiricism' in detail. The argument in this book is opposed to empiricism, and argues for the interrelationship of theory and observation.

FACTS AND THEORIES

We have deliberately avoided referring to 'facts' because the term implies something more than data or evidence. To assert that something is a fact implies that it is 'true' or 'correct' and that it has an existence somehow independent of the person asserting the 'fact' or the context within which it is situated. For example, to say that it is a fact that 20 per cent of the people of Britain live in poverty implies that the figure given is not only correct but that what constitutes 'living in poverty' is self-evident. Any such 'fact' depends on how you define 'poverty' and when and how you compile the data. In short, the 'fact' does not exist in isolation.

The implication when one talks of 'facts' is that they are bits of self-evident knowledge that exist irrespective of any values or theories. On the contrary, 'facts' are only 'facts' in relation to theory. We know a 'fact' because someone has made an 'observation' and linked it to a 'theory'. One may observe the sun rising in the east. This is an observation (and thus a datum or piece of evidence). This is not a 'fact' because we know that the Sun does not 'rise'; it stays still and the Earth moves. We know this because of many observations that make sense when linked to physical theories about moving bodies and astronomical theories about the vacuum of space.

This is what Chalmers (1994) referred to as the 'theory-laden nature of observation'. Observation does not provide us with self-evident 'facts', it provides us with bits of data or evidence and they make sense in relation to theories we have about the world.

Study point
Provide an example of how your observations of the social world are influenced by your existing theories or preconceptions.

Activity
Examine copies of the week's press (both broadsheet and tabloid) noting any headlines, articles or stories based on journalistic preconceptions. Explain what these might be.

VALUES IN THE RESEARCH PROCESS

It is a common assumption of science and everyday life that we can distinguish between 'facts' (what actually is) and values (what we think ought to be the case). Scientists and positivist sociologists argue that values should be excluded from science. However, it is by no means clear that it is possible to separate facts from values. Can we really assume that facts speak for themselves or do facts depend upon interpretation? For example, is it a fact that the Lennox Lewis/Evander Holyfield fight (1999) was a draw? Do all the people who watched the same fight agree on the outcome? If not, how can we come to a decision on who was the winner?

We need to ask ourselves whether it is really possible to rid ourselves of value judgements. That is, we need to ask if value-free research is possible. If we come to the conclusion that making value judgements is part of our human condition, then is it not pointless to try to eliminate values from the research process? If we come to the conclusion that it is pointless to try to eliminate values from the research process what should we do? May (1997) suggests that we should be turning the question round and asking what type of values do we base our judgements on? Using the example of the boxing match we could ask each judge on what basis they made their decision that the result of the fight was a draw. If, having asked this question we find the particular values in question wanting, we might wish to provide reasons why those values should be challenged. We could say the same thing of social research. Instead of assuming, as many scientists do, that research can be carried out in a value-free way, we could instead ask researchers to be as explicit as possible about the values that have influenced their research; indeed, this is what many sociologists do. In this way, we are able to understand the judgements that researchers make and we are able to understand our own reasons for accepting or rejecting them.

Researchers who acknowledge the role of values in research accept that different people in society have different interests. For example, we come from different cultural and historical backgrounds and our experiences are mediated by such things as our 'race', social class, gender, sexuality and ability or disability. We behave in ways that will be likely to further our interests. These interests affect the ways in which we define the problem or issue that we wish to research.

Nevertheless, some scientists and some sociologists would reject the view that research is value-laden. However, we know that scientific projects are sponsored by interested parties. This means that scientific activity is 'interested' as opposed to disinterested. This is not to say that the results from the piece of research will be worthless but it is to say that we should be aware of those issues that have influenced the piece of research for example; who funded the research? For what reason?

Finally, as power is not evenly distributed throughout society we need to ask questions about who has the power to construct certain issues as a problem in the first place. In other words, the values themselves become the focus of the research. Feminist researchers, for example, have pointed to the ways in which sexist and racist values have influenced the research process. Thus, we need to explore why some areas are selected as being of interest whilst others are not. We also need to explore the uses to which research may be put; often this may be far from the researcher's original intentions.

By now, it should be evident that the study of society involves researchers taking a value position on not only the topics that are to be researched but also on the ways in which research should be carried out. Even the dictum that science should be value-free is itself a value position. When we look at the relationship between theory and method we will see that our values influence the ways in which we do research.

RELATIONSHIP BETWEEN THEORY AND METHOD

There is a relationship between the theories of sociologists and the methods of study that they employ. 'Theory and method' together form the essential backbone of sociology. It is important, therefore, to see theory and method as different sides of the same coin. There is often a tendency in sociology textbooks to explore lots of theories without referring to method, to provide chapters on the theory of the family, organisations, deviance and so on and have a final chapter, rather like an appendix, that outlines different methods. This is misleading. It makes it appear that somehow sociology can be 'done' simply by theorising without any evidence. It also makes it appear as though 'methods' are simply techniques or tools that can be taken out of a toolbox and applied. This is not the case.

If, for example, you discover that your car windscreen wipers are loose on your car, you only need to find a spanner that fits the nut and tighten it up again. If, as a sociologist, you want to collect opinions from people, there is not a handy questionnaire that you can take out of a toolbox and go and use. You invariably have to design and test the appropriate instrument to see if it collects the opinions that you want. You might argue that it is nothing more than just a rather more complicated 'spanner'. However, the analogy falls apart because there is a stage before selecting the tool. When you have a loose nut it is just a matter of tightening it. When you want to get people's opinions it is not just a matter of asking questions, because, at the very least, the questions you ask will affect the information you get. The questions that you ask will be influenced by your values and prejudgements on the issue you are investigating.

For example, if you were studying the prevalence of HIV/AIDS your questions may be skewed by the erroneous preconception that the HIV virus primarily affects gay men. It may even be that asking questions is not appropriate because the kinds of things you want to know will not emerge from direct questioning. Furthermore, the way you interpret the answers may not be the same way as those who gave you the answers. Your interpretation may not even be the same as another sociologist because you may have different ways of looking at the world.

METHODOLOGY

It is important to distinguish methodology from method. Participant observation, in-depth interviewing, using postal questionnaires, re-analysing official statistics, are all examples of methods used in sociology. Methodology, however, involves specifying not just *how* you intend to collect evidence but *why*. Methodology also involves asking what is the relationship between the methods used to collect evidence and the explanation, interpretation or understanding that you are seeking. Methodology is about your whole approach to an area of research.

In short, there is a direct link between theory and method. The kind of issue you are interested in exploring and the sorts of things you are trying to find out will affect the methods you use. Conversely, the evidence that results from the methods you employ, and the way you interpret the evidence will impact on the theory that you develop.

So the way you do sociology involves more than just adopting a method and applying it to a theory. You need also to take into account the way you think about the world, what you regard as appropriate evidence, and the way that you define what constitutes sociological knowledge. Put simply, you need to be aware of your *methodology*.

CONFUSING DICHOTOMIES

There is a tendency, when introducing sociology, to create simple alternatives to help new students understand some of the complexities of social theory and methodology. These alternatives, or *dichotomies*, are used to show how one approach to sociology varies from another.

Some of the frequently used dichotomies are:

- quantitative versus qualitative;
- objective versus subjective;
- scientific versus non-scientific;
- rational versus emotional;
- positivistic versus phenomenological;
- explanation versus interpretation;
- structure versus action;
- conflict versus consensus.

Unfortunately, this approach to introducing sociology is ultimately more misleading than helpful. Often these dichotomies are grouped together to suggest, for example, that positivistic sociology uses quantitative methods to provide 'objective' explanations that are 'scientific', while phenomenological sociology provides 'subjective' interpretations that are 'non-scientific'. Another example is the way in which Durkheim and Marx are characterised as structural theorists whilst Weber is characterised as an action theorist. In reality, it is possible to see elements of both in the work of all three.

An analogy would be to characterise all the people you know as either:

- good or bad;
- clever or stupid;
- happy or miserable;
- deep or shallow;
- friendly or hostile.

and then suggest that you can divide your acquaintances into those who are friendly, happy, clever, deep and good or those who are hostile, miserable, stupid, shallow and bad.

Of course, life is more complicated than this and so is sociology. As we have seen, theorists make decisions about whether society can be treated as a reality that is external to the individual or as a reality that is socially created by the people who make up society. In the examples given above, it may appear as if Durkheim and Marx gave priority to society and that Weber gave priority to individual action. Certainly the ways in which they theorised about the nature of society and about the nature of 'science' may have given this impression but we must be careful to look at people's work as a whole.

Product or producer

Another tendency that misleads students new to sociology is to suppose that all the sociology undertaken by a particular sociologist is of the same sort.

So, for example, Émile Durkheim produced a study of suicide in which he undertook a comparative analysis of suicide statistics in Catholic and non-Catholic countries. He concluded that a higher degree of social isolation was, among other things, responsible for a higher suicide rate. Durkheim also wrote a small book on the method of social science in which he talked about social facts. As a result of these two texts Durkheim has become known as a *'positivistic'* sociologist, who used and proposed *quantitative methods* to provide social *explanations*. However, what tends to be overlooked when Durkheim is characterised as a 'positivist' is the work he did on religion. In this text he moved a long way from any 'scientific' approach to explore the fundamental nature of religious life. In short, we can say that not everything Durkheim produced was of the same type.

Generally, one should not refer to the individual sociologist as a positivist, phenomenologist, functionalist, Marxist, postmodernist or any other '-ist' and presume all the work he or she is involved in will fall into that category. That would be like calling Pablo Picasso a 'cubist' painter. Certainly, there was a period in his early career when he produced 'cubist' paintings but this lasted only a few years out of a lifetime's varied work.

Thus, it is important to explore individual pieces of work to see what presuppositions and theories lie behind them, what methods are used to collect information and what processes are used to draw conclusions. Just because a sociologist is labelled in a particular way it should not be assumed that the label is appropriate to all of her or his work.

COLLECTING EVIDENCE

Collecting data can be a haphazard or a systematic process. Haphazard data collection is whatever you happen to stumble across. Systematic data collection is based on a clearly stated method. In social science there are many methods that can be used to collect evidence including observation of events, interviewing people and searching through documents. There are many variations on these approaches and different circumstances require different forms of investigation, as you will see in the examples in the following chapters. A method can be used in many different settings and for a variety of purposes. Also some tools or methods are better for some jobs than others.

Methods are of two broad types. *Primary* methods involve researchers collecting their own data. They may, of course, have help to do this, such as hiring interviewers. The data they collect is 'new'. That is, it is either completely new, such as a taped interview with someone. Or it is material that already exists but is 'collected' and used in a new way, such as the videoing of television news broadcasts for analysis of political bias.

Secondary methods involve reanalysing information that has already been used as part of a research study. This includes the following:

- using a database of information collected for one study for a new but related study;
- using official statistics collected by government agencies (for example on poverty and on unemployment) as evidence in exploring the relationship between poverty and unemployment;
- using data archives to collect information from a range of studies to undertake a comparative study;
- search the published literature to collect evidence to examine a theory.

Most social research involves a mixture of primary and secondary methods. Researchers usually explore the existing literature to find out what other studies have shown about the area of research. Most, although not all, research also involves some 'new' material that the researcher has collected.

Primary research takes three broad forms:

1   asking questions;
2   observation;
3   'document' analysis.

In the latter case, a 'document' is not necessarily something written or printed on paper. It can include 'aural documents' such as tape recordings, visual documents such as video, films, paintings or any other collection of material, even in one famous research study, the collection of rubbish from people's dustbins (Sawyer, 1961). What we have called 'document analysis' is sometimes referred to as 'unobtrusive methods' because it involves using material that does not involve any direct intrusion into the lives of the subjects of the research.

The wide range of methods of data collection are summarised in the following tables.

METHOD	ACTIVITY	PURPOSE
	Table 2.2: *Primary data collection: asking questions*	
Conversations	Asking questions as part of casual conversations.	To get some preliminary idea of the extent of an activity or the perceptions of people.
Key-informant discussion	A discussion (or series of discussions) with someone who is particularly well informed about the research area.	To get rapidly acquainted with aspects of the research area, discover what is known or taken-for-granted and which areas need further research, develop contacts, learn appropriate language, etc.
In-depth interviews	Spending time asking a series of linked but open questions. Gently probing answers to get more detail. Being flexible to allow respondent to explore their concerns.	To identify the key concerns of respondents and/or to obtain as much subtle detail as possible about activities or perceptions.
Semi-structured interviews	Similar to in-depth interviews but usually with a more narrowly defined brief and a clearer set of topics to be covered during the interview.	To obtain information about a specified range of areas determined by the researcher but flexible enough to pursue interesting avenues raised by the respondent.
Formal structured interviews	Making use of a pre-set interview schedule to ensure all respondents are asked the same questions in the same order and given the same prompts.	To collect responses, from a sample, to a predetermined set of questions in such a way that 'representative' statistical analysis can be carried out on the results to provide an indication of the extent of certain kinds of activity or preponderance of particular views.
Structured (mainly open response) questionnaires	Using a questionnaire with a set of open questions with the hope of encouraging respondents to provide details about actions, requirements or perceptions.	Rather like semi-structured interviews, used when the sample is too large for direct contact, but usually with very much more limited information.
Structured (mainly closed response or tick-box') questionnaires	Using a questionnaire with a set of pre-determined answers, from which respondents select the answer that most closely reflects their activity or views.	A similar aim to that of formal structured interviews. Used when the sample is too large or too spread out to be able to deploy interviewers to collect data.
Informal group discussions	Using a group situation to explore a range of issues.	Usually undertaken to get an indication of both the group perspective and the differences within the group. Sometimes an opportunistic event making the most of having an appropriate group of 'key informants' in one place.

Table continued on subsequent page

Table 2.2: *Primary data collection: asking questions (continued)*

METHOD	ACTIVITY	PURPOSE
Focus groups	A formal process of group discussion and feedback that takes many forms. One approach is to ask each individual to spend a very short time writing down some key points about the area of concern to the researcher. This is followed by small group discussions where respondents pool ideas and develop a small group perspective. This is then followed by a period in which the small groups take turns to present their views to the whole group. Finally a whole group discussion takes place.	Aim is to collect opinions or reflections on activity from a large group in a relatively efficient manner. Furthermore, the interactive aspect of this approach allows ideas to develop, or latent views to emerge that might, in individual interviews, have remained dormant.
Life history / biography method	Using a combination of methods including a series of in-depth or semi-structured interviews, plus asking respondents to write down significant events or perceptions. (This is not always restricted to the construction of a life history or biography.)	The aim is to identify the evolution of an individual's experiences or practices or to identify how or why changes in activity or perceptions came about.

© LEE HARVEY.

Table 2.3: *Primary data collection: observing events*

METHOD	ACTIVITY	PURPOSE
Overheard	Hanging about being inquisitive.	To get some preliminary idea of the perceptions of people.
Casual, *ad hoc* observation	Observing activities when the opportunity arises.	To get some preliminary idea of the extent of an activity or the way people perceive things.
Structured observation	Undertaking systematic observation of specified situations.	To get a more representative view of the way people behave or construct their meanings.
Diagnostic observation (spying)	Observation of people in a contrived setting or situation, such as a group of people on the other side of a one-way mirror being observed to see how they interact in a group.	As a tool to explore behaviour or the meanings that people have, or as an experimental tool to see how people react when the contrived situation is changed.

Table continued on subsequent page

Table 2.3: *Primary data collection: observing events (continued)*

METHOD	ACTIVITY	PURPOSE
Shadowing	Following someone around, usually with his or her permission.	To obtain first-hand knowledge of the person's experiences. Often used when trying to find out what someone's job is like.
Complete secret participant observer	Observation that occurs when a researcher joins a group as an active member, to observe the group activity, without telling anyone about the research purpose.	To get an insider view of the activities, views and attitudes of members of the group.
Complete open participant observer	Observation that occurs when a researcher joins a group as an active member, to observe the group activity, but is open about the research purpose.	To get an insider view of the activities, views and attitudes of members of the group, without running the risk of being found out or asked to do something illegal or morally unacceptable.
Partial secret participant observation	Observation that occurs when a researcher spends some time with a group or in a social setting, to observe activity, without telling anyone about the research purpose.	To get a close view of the activities that occur in a setting and the perspectives of the social actors without the need to become a full-time member of a group.
Partial open participant observation	Observation that occurs when a researcher spends some time with a group or in a social setting, to observe activity, but is open about the research purpose.	To get a close view of the activities that occur in a setting and the perspectives of the social actors without the need to become a full-time member of a group and without running the risk of being found out or asked to do something illegal or morally unacceptable.
Associate member participant observation	Hanging around with a group of people, without becoming a member, in order to observe activities. For example, an adult community leader hanging around with a group of adolescents.	To get a close-up view of the activities, views and attitudes of members of the group.

\multicolumn{3}{c}{Table 2.4: *Primary data collection: analysing documents** }
METHOD	ACTIVITY	PURPOSE
Literature search	Searching through available published material (books, journals, newspapers, etc.) often using databases or abstracts in libraries.	To get background information on what is already 'known' about the particular area of sociology. This also provides information on theories that have been used and studies that have been undertaken. Most research starts here.
Document/ archive exploration	A close analysis of the content of unpublished (or 'grey' literature) or other archives, such as working documents, drafts, minutes of meetings, letters, diaries.	To collect information or get insights about the operation of individuals, groups or organisations, from material not usually in the public domain.
Document analysis	An intensive analysis of what lies behind the ostensive content of documents.	An attempt to explore the motives or underlying ideas of, or constraints placed on, the author of a 'document'.
Content analysis	A process of counting up the frequency of occurrence of specific words or phrases or accounts within a document, such as in a newspaper article.	To try and provide a quantitative indicator of the frequency of occurrence of a particular subject with a view to relating it to other factors.
Semiotics	A close scrutiny of the relationship between a 'linguistic' sign (such as a word), what it denotes and the connotations that it conveys in a particular context.	To get beneath the surface of sign systems or messages to discover the underlying ideology.
Iconography	Similar to semiology, a close scrutiny of the 'icons' being used in a picture, film or television script (for example).	To explore how images convey (taken-for granted) messages or underlying ideology.
Narrative analysis/ film 'study'	Narrative analysis examines the way that a narrative is developed (often as part of a film), what its key elements are and how devices are used to convey a meaning.	To explore the underlying meanings or ideology of the makers of the film and how they engage with, or reproduce, prevailing social norms and values.
Glossing (ethnomethod-ology)	Microscopic examination of the meanings of everyday words by examining them in the context in which they appear (known as 'indexicality').	To try and construct the specific meaning of words to show how meaning is developed through interaction.

Table continued on subsequent page

Table 2.4: *Primary data collection: analysing documents* (continued)		
METHOD	ACTIVITY	PURPOSE
Conversation analysis	A microscopic analysis of conversation, usually recorded and transcribed including the words, accentuation used and pauses.	To explore how people make sense of their everyday interactions, or what taken-for-granted concepts they have in common with other people, or how prevailing concepts structure their conversations.

*A 'document' may be paper-based, video, picture, painting or any other cultural object or recorded conversation. This is also sometimes called unobtrusive methods.

© LEE HARVEY

Activity

List five methods you would consider using if you wanted to find out under what circumstances the police would make an arrest. Consider some of the advantages and disadvantages of each.

THE 'SOCIOLOGICAL TRADITION': DURKHEIM, MARX AND WEBER

Let's look, for the moment, at some examples of early sociologists' work so that you can see how different theorists at particular times have put their theories about science and society into practice. We will demonstrate the linkage between these theories and the methods that were used.

DURKHEIM

Durkheim, in his book *Rules of Sociological Method*, talks about 'social facts'. We would usually refer to social facts as 'the rules of behaviour that we learn' and through which we organise our lives. Such rules or conventions may vary from culture to culture. Durkheim states that these social facts are both external to us and constrain what we do. What he means by this is that the rules of society are already in existence when we are born. We learn to live by these rules and we also learn the consequences of breaking them. In a sense we can thus be said to be 'determined' by society.

What this shows is that Durkheim was concerned with social order. It also shows that Durkheim assumed that human beings are in need of constraint. This indicates that, at this point in his writings, he may have assumed that it is the nature of humans to act selfishly.

These assumptions influenced Durkheim's thinking about what was the best way to produce knowledge about society. If it is accepted that the rules of society can be seen to *cause* human beings to act in particular ways, then it is logical to accept that the best way of producing knowledge about society is to copy the methods of natural science, which seeks to find causes or natural 'laws'. Thus, it is assumed that the 'laws of society' can be discovered in much the same way as the 'laws of nature'. Durkheim's work, particularly *Suicide*, provides an early exemplar of positivist research (see Chapter 3).

MARX

Marx looked at the way in which societies have developed in relation to the economic mode of production that they have adopted. Through Marx's extensive study of history and society, for example *Das Kapital*, he concluded that societies throughout history have largely been characterised by conflict. The conflict has arisen because the economic modes of production have been based upon unfair and exploitative class relationships. Marx was particularly concerned to show how in the capitalist mode of production in particular, the exploitation of the workers by the ruling class is hidden. He did this by revealing the theoretical mechanisms through which systems of domination are maintained. This is known as a 'critical' approach to the social world. As a result of this process, Marx was of the view that the working class would become conscious of their exploitation and as a result they would act to produce social change which would bring about a fairer society (communism). (This is explored in more detail in Chapter 5.)

KARL MARX

Here we can see that Marx assumes that human nature can be both selfish and unselfish. He also assumes that under the capitalist mode of production society is in a sense external to the individuals within it. However, at the same time, he assumes that once individuals understand the processes through which the structures of society are maintained, they can act upon society to bring about change. This means that Marx saw the need to go beyond the positivist concern with that which can be observed, to focus upon those aspects of life that cannot be observed. That is, we are again able to see that there is a relationship between theorists' assumptions about the nature of their subject matter and their assumptions about the most appropriate way to produce knowledge.

WEBER

In a similar vein to Marx, Weber was also deeply critical of capitalism. In his study *The Protestant Ethic and the Spirit of Capitalism*, Weber's analysis begins with a focus on the meaning of individual actions rather than on the economic structure upon which capitalist society rests. In particular, Weber argued that it was the beliefs of those who belonged to the Calvinist faith that provided the conditions that were necessary for capitalism to develop. Calvinists were encouraged to be industrious and at the same time to be frugal. This combination of ideas was important to the development of capitalism because, for it to succeed, capital had to be accumulated (that is, capitalism is built on investment). The rationale behind the original actions of the Calvinists was their need to secure their salvation. As a result of the belief that God would only allow those who were worthy to prosper in life, Calvinists focused on what Weber calls 'goal-oriented action' to convince themselves that they were chosen by God to be saved. Thus the focus on the most efficient means to ends, which characterises the drive for profit in capitalist societies, was, according to Weber, a direct result of the development of Calvinism.

Here we can see that Weber, unlike Durkheim and Marx, began from the assumption that society is meaningfully created by individuals. This led him to the assumption that the most appropriate way to gain knowledge about the social world was through interpretive understanding (*Verstehen*) of the ways in which actions produced social structures. For this reason, Weber is referred to as an 'action theorist'. This aspect of Weber's work represented a clear break with positivism because positivists consider interpretation to be outside the boundaries of 'scientific' enquiry. It is also this aspect of Weber's work that led to the development of *phenomenological* sociology (Chapter 4).

It can be seen that Weber's analysis leads to far more pessimistic conclusions than that of Marx. As we saw, Marx believed that theoretical understanding could lead to actions that would produce a fairer society. Although Weber's analysis begins with the seemingly unselfish actions of individuals, these actions have, albeit unintentionally, given rise to a constraining social system that is characterised by instrumental rationality. Furthermore, Weber ends up concluding that there is no escape from this bureaucratic way of life. We can see that although Weber's analysis may have attempted to demonstrate that society is created by individuals, his assumption that modern industrial society is, above all else, characterised by instrumental rationality, has led to the negation of human action.

Activity

How far do you think that your life experiences are determined by factors that are external to you? Discuss your answers with other members of your class.

RECENT DEVELOPMENTS

In recent years, sociologists have attempted to overcome some of the oppositional ways of thinking to which we have referred above. Reflecting the concerns of phenomenologists, Anthony Giddens is of the view that the nature of society is completely different to the nature of the objects of natural science.

1 Giddens, therefore, challenges Durkheim's call to treat social facts as things. Human beings are thinking and feeling subjects who cannot (and should not) be treated like inanimate objects.

2 Giddens has also suggested that it is more useful to think of 'action' and 'structure' as inseparable, rather than as a dichotomy. Such an acknowledgement avoids the view that human beings are determined, in a puppet-like fashion, by factors that are external to them, whilst also accepting that actions are often constrained by the production and reproduction of certain social institutions.

3 This acknowledgement also takes account of the main criticism of phenomenology, that is, that it pays too little attention to the material conditions in which social life takes place.

Feminists, from a variety of perspectives, also endorse the view that the human sciences need to involve interpretation. However, they add:

1 That, in presenting itself as the highest form of knowledge, science oppresses women. This is because science has tended to separate the rational from the emotional aspects of life.

2 Linked to this separation is the (false) assumption that men are rational and women are emotional.

3 The positivistic belief that science should ignore values and emotion is thus a reason for many women to reject it as an adequate model for sociology.

Postmodernists give up the idea of finding a theory of society at all. This is because:

1 They reject the possibility of finding 'the truth'. As we will see in Chapter 5, some postmodernists argue that science is apparently 'true' because it is powerful, not powerful because it is true.

2 However, as Chalmers argues, such an 'anything goes' account of science might in practice lead to the maintenance of the *status quo*. This is because the postmodernist position can lead to 'relativism' in which one 'truth' becomes as good as any other.

Such criticisms of postmodernism have led to a renewed interest in 'critical realism'.

1 Critical realism rejects the view that science should be limited to that which can be directly observed. There may be structures in society that exist but of which we are not necessarily conscious. This is an ontological assumption (see above). As Cain (1993) argues, this is a separate issue from the question of how far we can find out the truth about these structures.

2 Critical realism does not accept that one 'truth' is as good as any other, rather it seeks to provide reasons why some views may be better for society than others.

SUMMARY

Thinking sociologically requires us to develop theories and compare them with our experiences and observations of the world.

* Theorising about society requires that we actively seek out evidence to help us develop and substantiate our theories.
* Theoretical assumptions are made about the nature of society; these are called *ontological* assumptions.
* Sociologists also need to make decisions about the most appropriate way to produce knowledge; these are called *epistemological* decisions.
* 'Theory' is a term that covers a variety of levels of theorising: specific theories, broader perspectives and sociological research traditions.

We can sum up 'theorising' diagrammatically as follows:

Figure 2.1: Theorising

Theorising	→ about the nature of society	→ ontology
	→ about how to produce knowledge	→ epistemology
Research traditions	→ positivism phenomenology critical	→ Durkheim → Weber → Marx
Perspectives	→ functionalism radical feminism etc.	
Specific theories	→ labelling theory etc.	

Sociologists need to develop *methods* to collect evidence to support or challenge theories. Method refers to the tools used to collect data or evidence. These include:

- primary methods such as observation, questionnaires, in-depth interviews, conversational analysis;
- secondary methods such as re-analysing official statistics.

Methods, as tools, can be used in a variety of different sociological approaches.

'Theory and method' are interrelated and are two sides of the same coin.

- The key to social research is to obtain a balance between 'data' and 'theory'.
- Observation does not provide us with self-evident 'facts', it provides us with bits of data or evidence and they make sense in relation to theories we have about the world.
- It is important to distinguish methodology from method. Method is a tool and methodology is an approach which involves specifying not just *how* you intend to collect evidence but *why*.

We can sum up the relationship between method and methodology diagrammatically as follows:

Figure 2.2: Method and methodology

Methods	→ Ways of collecting data	→ Primary e.g, interviews, questionnaires, observation
		→ Secondary e.g, documents, official statistics
Methodology	→ *Why* collect evidence?	→ What is the link between theories and methods?

We have questioned the common assumption that we can distinguish between facts and values.

We have shown that the works of Durkheim, Marx and Weber are influenced by their particular values, ontological and epistemological assumptions.

Recent developments in sociology have questioned some of the traditional dichotomies evident in much sociology.

STUDY GUIDE

Group Work

Task 1:

Make 13 cards on which each has one of the concepts listed in Table 2.1. The cards are dealt to each member of the group. Each person should then work out the best possible definition of each concept using the text or other sources. The definitions are to be written on another blank card. All the cards are collected and shuffled. Each one is read out (either a concept or a definition). The group then test their ability to recognise and define concepts.

Task 2:

Similar to task 1, members make a set of cards listing the methods of producing data (see Tables 2.2, 2.3 and 2.4). Cards are shuffled and dealt. Each person gives an example of a research project that could be undertaken using the method written on the card. Each project is read out and the group then discuss which method they think would be applicable. This is compared with the method that the project was supposed to illustrate.

Exam Hint

Check past papers to see the frequency with which questions on methods occur. Note the range of questions that are asked.

Revision Hints (applicable to all chapters)

Reread the chapter.

1 Make a list of all the sub-headings used in this chapter. Test your understanding by writing as much as possible under each heading without making reference to any texts.
2 Pick out some key concepts, for example epistemology. Try to write out definitions. Where possible, try to make connections between other concepts, for example ontology. Describe the differences between the concepts.
3 Make summary cards listing key concepts and issues used in this chapter.
4 Make cards listing the names of key sociologists mentioned in this chapter with brief details of their significance and contribution.

Revision Hints

1 To what extent is the choice of method in research influenced by theory?
2 What factors influence sociologists in their choice of methods?
3 Distinguish between primary and secondary sources of data.
4 Are observation studies more useful than large-scale surveys?

3

THE NATURE OF SCIENCE: POSITIVISM

THINKING POSITIVISTICALLY

POSITIVISM IS ONE way of knowing the social world. Positivism attempts to apply a natural scientific approach to the study of the social world. The approach seeks to identify cause-and-effect relationships. It is assumed that for each social phenomenon there is a social cause.

Some versions of positivism assume that the only evidence that we can accept is that which we can perceive with our senses. You will remember from Chapter 2 that this is called empiricism. However, not all research that comes under the label 'positivist' is empiricist.

Positivism also assumes that we can rid ourselves of any preconceptions that we might have in order to produce 'factual' information.

In summary, positivist approaches to the social world:

- use sense data (that is, evidence that is observable or otherwise grasped through our senses);
- seek cause-and-effect relationships;
- attempt to be value-free.

CONTEXT IN WHICH SOCIOLOGY EMERGED

To understand the debates surrounding the question of whether sociology should be a science or not, it is necessary to examine the context in which sociology emerged as an academic discipline. The early sociologists, to whom we

Table 3.1: *Key concepts and questions in this chapter*	
KEY CONCEPTS	KEY QUESTIONS
Cause-and-effect relationships	Can there be one social cause for each social phenomenon?
Value freedom	Can social research be neutral?
Enlightenment thinking	What is the social significance of the enlightenment?
Induction	What are the key differences between
Deduction	induction and deduction?
Falsificationism	Why might falsificationism be said to be more logical than induction?
Paradigms	Is science carried out in a social framework?
Operationalisation	How can we change a concept into a measurable variable?
Validity (as understood in positivism)	Does the data being collected actually measure the concept being investigated?
Reliability	Can research be reliable yet invalid?
Representative	Does the data represent the population it is supposed to represent?
Variables	What is the difference between dependent and independent variables? What is the direction of the causal link?
Generalisation	Are the findings from the research sample convincing enough to make wider claims about all people who fit into the group under study?

referred in the previous chapter, were trying to make sense of the rapid social changes that characterised the transition from traditional, agricultural societies to modern industrial societies. In the former, there was very little sense of individuality, as we know it today, because most tasks were carried out in groups. Modern society, on the other hand, was one in which tasks became increasingly divided and specialised.

These changes brought about the development of an intellectual tradition that challenged the faith in religious knowledge as the way to understand the world. Instead, there was a move to raise the status of science. A group of French and Scottish social thinkers argued for a rational approach as a way of challenging the power of both religious leaders and kings. This 'enlightenment' thinking, as it was called, was radical in its time. It promised a shift from the seemingly fixed social positions, in which some people were assured of continued wealth and power and others were doomed to poverty. In traditional societies, these inequalities were largely explained in terms of 'the will of God'. The belief in the power of this new 'scientific' reasoning was, therefore, understandably seen as a way in which society could be changed for the better.

Enlightenment thinkers challenged knowledge that was taken for granted. As Fuller (1997) argues, the sociological function of enlightenment thinking was to challenge the existing social order. The way of thinking, that was seen to be typical of science, was open to anyone, not just élite groups (such as priests). However, although enlightenment thinking was 'radical' in some respects it was mainly concerned with greater freedoms for particular groups of (white) men. There was little concern, for example, amongst the 'philosophes' (as these thinkers were called) for women and black people.

There was a fear that in a modern world of increased specialisation society would become disorderly. Thus positivism, the science that was advocated by early sociologists, aimed to bring consensus to society. The positivistic view of science assumed that it would be carried out by 'experts' who would know what was best for society. The main purpose of these experts would be to justify particular courses of action by providing empirical evidence.

We should not really be surprised that early sociologists accepted this view since, as Bauman (1990) suggests, a new discipline would need to secure public recognition and approval and one way of doing this was to assert that sociology could be used to improve the human condition. In Bauman's (1990, p 218) words: 'The pressure to conform to the standard established by natural sciences was enormous and virtually impossible to resist.'

Fuller (1997) argues that the primary concern of enlightenment thinkers was freedom from the constraints of 'mindlessly reproduced tradition'. In contrast, he sees the early positivist sociologist, Auguste Comte (the man who first coined the term 'sociology'), as primarily concerned with restoring order to society.

THE 'SCIENTIFIC METHOD'

Positivists tend to refer to their approach to *the study of society* as 'the scientific method'. However, although positivism attempts to uncover cause-and-effect relationships, there are disagreements among positivists as to the ways in which this can be achieved. In short, they disagree about what constitutes 'the scientific method'. For some, positivist science depends on an *inductive* method, for others it is based on *deduction*.

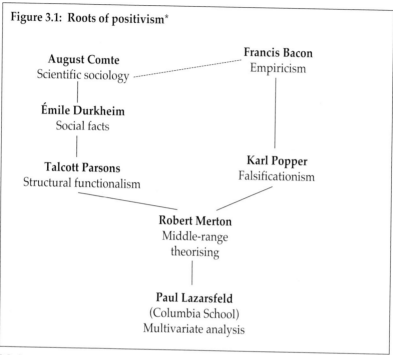

Figure 3.1: Roots of positivism*

August Comte — Scientific sociology
Francis Bacon — Empiricism
Émile Durkheim — Social facts
Talcott Parsons — Structural functionalism
Karl Popper — Falsificationism
Robert Merton — Middle-range theorising
Paul Lazarsfeld — (Columbia School) Multivariate analysis

* Only people referred to in the text are included in this diagram.
© LEE HARVEY

Study point

Write down what you consider to be the key characteristics of science. Compare your answer with the two versions (inductivism and deductivism) below.

INDUCTIVE SCIENCE

Francis Bacon, an early seventeenth-century thinker, believed that the purpose of science was to improve the human condition. He set out a way of doing science that involved the collection of 'facts'. For Bacon, facts were to be collected through careful recording of observations following which it is possible to make an observation statement. The key assumption here is that it is possible for researchers to rid themselves of all preconceptions in order to record 'the facts'. Say, for example, we decided to study people with red hair. We might, following lots of observations, state that 'the redheads observed in places A, B and C at times F, G and H, all had freckles'. We could check whether this is true or not by carrying out more careful observations. Eventually, having observed redheads in many places and at various times we could then make a universal statement 'all redheads have freckles'. This view of science is called inductivist science. Chalmers (1994, p 5) sums up the principle of induction in the following way: 'If a large number of As have been observed under a wide variety of conditions and if all those observed As without exception possessed the property B, all As have the property B.'

We can thus see that inductive reasoning is a process of generalisation from particular observations to general statements. The data, therefore, is assumed to precede theories. Put more simply, this approach assumes that researchers can discover certain knowledge by finding more and more evidence to support their theories.

Activity
Working in pairs, choose a location such as a fast-food outlet. Independently write down your observations of the people going in. Compare your observations with those made by your partner. Do your written observations suggest that you have observed the same thing? Do these observations provide you with the basis for conclusions about the types of people who use fast-food outlets? What does this tell you about the role of theory in observation?

As we have said, an inductivist view of science implies that theories are developed from facts. Having carried out your observation do you agree? Or do you think that when you observe something you bring your existing theoretical knowledge to that which you observe?

DEDUCTIVE SCIENCE

Deduction begins from the opposite direction to induction. Those who utilise a deductive method acknowledge the role of theory at the start of their research. That is, deductivists challenge the view that data precedes theory. Deductivism involves a process of elaborating theory by deducing relationships and then exploring whether the evidence confirms them. In practice, in social research, the predominant positivist approach is based on a version of deductivism known as *falsificationism*.

Falsificationism

In the 1930s, the philosopher of science, Karl Popper (1980), pointed out the mistaken logic of inductivism. First, it is not possible to rid ourselves of our preconceptions when we observe (as you may by now have found out). Second, Popper argued that no matter how many times we verify something we can never assert that we have reached the 'truth' because the next observation may prove us wrong. He used the example of swans: the statement 'all swans are white' was refuted when the black swan was observed in Australia. The conclusion 'all swans are white', derived from many observations of white swans in different times and places, is 'false' even though the premises are 'true'.

Therefore, Popper suggested an alternative version of science known as falsificationism in which more limited claims are made. For example, once a black swan has been observed we can come to the more limited conclusion that not all swans are white. This is more logical than inductivism because both the premise (a black swan) and the conclusion (not all swans are white) are true.

This means that instead of trying to make theories fit the facts, as in induction, Popper acknowledges that facts are derived from theories. Popper was concerned that researchers should subject themselves to critique. In order to do this he believed that it was appropriate that they should maximise their chances of being proved wrong by making statements that, at least in principle, are capable of being falsified. This avoids the situation in which researchers simply go out to find data that confirms their theories. This can be seen as a rejection of the early positivist project of seeking universal laws. Theories that remain unfalsified are the best we can have for now. This is not the same as saying that they are true for all time. The falsificationist view of science is that science is made up of the theoretical statements that have not been *disproved*. Falsificationism can also be seen as a rejection of the view that sense experience is the only basis of scientific knowledge.

Popper's work was important because it demonstrated that theories inform data. However, as we shall see in the following chapters, this is not the end of the debate. As sociologists, you will need to ask yourselves why you would want to let go of a theory simply because it was falsified. Many scientists have made important discoveries precisely because they have ignored falsifying evidence. You might also want to ask why Popper did not recognise that the acceptance of the falsifying evidence is ultimately dependent upon the researcher's interpretation of that evidence. That is, we are returned to a key problem with induction because observation does not occur in a theory-free way and all observation statements are fallible (see Chapter 2 on the theory-related nature of observation).

PARADIGMS

If we look at the ways in which natural scientists carry out their work we can see that, in practice, they use both inductive *and* deductive methods. Indeed, if natural scientists had abandoned their theories each time they were presented with falsifying evidence then there would be very little scientific theory. Debates in the philosophy of science have shown how the positivistic version of science has been attacked from within science itself. This means that those who argue that social science should copy natural science may be operating with a conception of natural science that many scientists would now reject (Delanty, 1997).

Thomas Kuhn (1970), for example, examined the ways in which scientists carry out their research. He argued that science takes place within a framework of rules (called a 'paradigm') to which all scientists adhere. Science is a communal activity, not an individual one. Therefore, scientists share assumptions which tend to remain unquestioned. Kuhn identified four phases of science:

1 pre-science;
2 normal science;
3 revolutionary science;
4 new normal science.

In the first phase, many competing frameworks operate. A dominant framework emerges, which becomes the 'normal' scientific mode. This model then becomes the exemplar for all scientific work. This becomes the dominant paradigm. Scientists operate normally within the framework of the dominant paradigm and it is difficult to challenge the framework. This is because the community of scientists take the dominant framework for granted. Kuhn argued that paradigms only break down when it becomes impossible to solve the current problems within that framework. This takes quite a long time to occur because when scientists achieve unexpected results they usually assume that they have made mistakes rather than questioning the framework itself. It is only when there are so many anomalies, which can no longer be ignored, that scientists as a community begin to develop alternative frameworks. This shift takes place when some scientists develop a new set of theories and concepts outside the existing paradigm. This revolutionary phase eventually settles down as the new normal scientific paradigm.

Popper's version of science, whilst rejecting certainty, nevertheless retains the view that we edge ever closer towards 'the truth'. Kuhn is arguing that the shift from one paradigm to another represents a complete shift in a conceptual framework.

Positivism thus asserts that science is powerful because it leads to truth. Kuhn's version of science asserts that science is powerful because it is useful. Once the concepts and theories in use fail to help us to solve 'puzzles' new ones take their place. What we once considered to be true becomes false within the context of the new paradigm.

We will return to the philosophical debates about the nature of knowledge throughout the book.

The best way to gain a clearer understanding of the assumptions made in positivistic sociology is to examine a piece of research which has been carried out within this tradition. In this way you will be in a better position to judge for yourself how far you think that positivism is appropriate to the study of society.

DURKHEIM'S STUDY OF SUICIDE: INDUCTIVE OR DEDUCTIVE?

We have already suggested that it is not wise to assume that all the work carried out by one person is of the same sort. Durkheim's work on suicide, however, was the study through which he put his science of society into operation and it is generally held to be an exemplar of positivist sociology. The assumption is that, as Durkheim emphasised 'social facts', the approach he adopted is primarily *inductive*.

Despite the seemingly individual nature of the act of suicide, Durkheim was concerned to find out what were the structural reasons for suicide. He was saying that individual or psychological explanations were inadequate because, although individuals actually commit the act of killing themselves, the causes are social and therefore external to individuals.

The first thing that Durkheim did in his study was to examine the official statistics on suicide in 11 European countries. His careful examination of the similarities and differences in the suicide rates in the various countries led him to three main conclusions:

1 within any given society the rates of suicide are surprisingly constant over time;
2 the rate varies between societies;
3 the rate varies between different groups within the same societies.

In attempting to find the social causes of suicide, Durkheim carried out his study in a similar way to the way in which scientists in a laboratory would carry out their work. For example, Durkheim observed from the statistical evidence, that suicide was more prevalent in Protestant countries than in Catholic ones. However, this information alone could not tell him that being Protestant is important. To show that being Protestant was important Durkheim attempted to discount other possible factors. For example, Germany, a largely Protestant country, had higher rates of suicide than Italy, a Catholic country. Perhaps nationality could be a factor causing suicide? To test this, Durkheim examined the different regions within Germany and he found that Bavaria, a region with the largest number of Catholics, had the least number of suicides. This confirmed Durkheim's theory that religion was an important factor.

Durkheim also noticed that people who were married were less likely to commit suicide than those who were not, and that people with children were less likely to commit suicide than those who did not have children. As a result of all these factors he suggested that one social *cause* of suicide was a lack of integration in society. He called the type of suicide resulting from lack of integration *egoistic* suicide. He concluded that religion, marriage and children were all factors that would be likely to integrate people in society. He theorised that the Catholic and Jewish religions were more integrative and family-oriented than Protestant religions, therefore this would explain lower suicide rates. Durkheim surmised that increases in suicide rates in general could be *explained* by the transition from the more integrated traditional societies to the less integrated modern industrial societies in which social bonds were breaking down.

Using the same approach, Durkheim concluded that there were three other forms of suicide. When the rules of normal behaviour break down people become in a state of normlessness (that is, they become unsure of the rules of society). Durkheim called this *anomie* and he, therefore, argued that *anomic* suicide occurs because of a lack of regulation in society. This along with egoistic suicide is the type of suicide that is likely in modern societies.

Altruistic suicide occurs when people are too integrated in society, when their sense of solidarity outweighs their concern for themselves. As a result of this over-integration individuals may sacrifice themselves for the greater good of the group to which they belong. Finally *fatalistic* suicide occurs when the rules of society are so strong that people feel stifled and unable to develop a sense of self.

We can see that Durkheim assumed that society is a reality that is *external* to individuals' consciousness. The suicide statistics provide the raw data; they are the *social facts* that are used in the research. Although Durkheim claimed to be following his own rules of sociological method, in which theories are subsequent to the observation of the data, it is debatable whether Durkheim has proceeded inductively from the facts of suicide to the social causes of suicide.

So, although Durkheim was attempting to put into operation a value-free science, that is, a science in which facts and values are assumed to be separable, his own assumptions and preconceptions about the transition from traditional to modern societies influenced the way in which he analysed the suicide statistics. Thus, Durkheim was not limiting his enquiry to things that are capable of being directly observed. Durkheim did not simply go out and collect 'facts' about rates of suicide, he theorised about the possible factors that might lead to suicide.

FUNCTIONALISM

Durkheim's theoretical assumptions in his study on suicide can be seen to be linked directly to his concern for social cohesion. These concerns were also evident in his work *The Division of Labour in Society*, in which Durkheim argued that it is possible to make a direct analogy between the way in which our bodies work and the way in which society should function. Each part of the body needs to function properly for us to be healthy. Similarly, each part of society, according to Durkheim, needs to function in ways that contribute to the greater good of society as a whole.

This approach came to be referred to as *functionalism*. Durkheim's theorising about the factors leading to suicide, for example, suggest that 'the family' functions to integrate people into the values of society. It can be seen that this is in line with Durkheim's view, at least at this point in his career, that society is external to individuals.

STRUCTURAL FUNCTIONALISM

The American sociologist, Talcott Parsons, further developed Durkheim's ideas in *The Social System* (1951). In this text, Parsons outlined what he considered to be the four basic prerequisites for a functional society. His view that society is a system into which people are socialised is the essence of *structural functionalism*, according to which view society is considered to be greater than the sum of its parts. For structural functionalists society is a *system* of interlocking parts that all have a function in sustaining society.

Robert Merton, a contemporary of Parsons, developed structural functionalism by distinguishing between manifest (clear or evident) functions and latent (hidden) functions. For example, a functioning family will produce children who conform to the accepted norms of society: this is a manifest function. Nevertheless, crime in society serves the latent function of revealing the socially accepted limits of behaviour.

The main argument against structural functionalism is that it simply justifies the *status quo*. It is assumed that just because some things have existed for a long time they must be serving an important function. As we will see in Chapter 5, such a view fails to take account of differential access to power and wealth in society.

ELEMENTS OF THE POSITIVISTIC APPROACH TO SOCIOLOGY

Despite these disagreements about the precise nature of 'the scientific method', most positivist sociologists agree with the following basic elements of the positivistic approach.

For most positivist sociologists, the development of theory is via a process of making assertions (known as hypotheses) about the relationship between two or more factors and then testing whether these assertions can be 'falsified' when data is collected and analysed. The process of falsifying requires that 'appropriate' data is collected and that all theoretically sensible explanations of the relationship between the factors are tested out to make sure that they really do relate to each other. Paul Lazarsfeld and his colleagues at the University of Columbia (collectively referred to as the Columbia School) have clearly set out the positivistic approach to sociology (Lazarsfeld and Rosenberg, 1955; Lazarsfeld, Pasanella and Rosenberg, 1972).

The elements are as follows:

1 reviewing existing theory and establishing a hypothesis;
2 operationalising concepts;
3 collecting data;
4 testing the hypothesis using multivariate analysis;
5 generalising from the results and suggesting changes to theory and new hypotheses to test.

THEORY AND HYPOTHESES

A theory, as we have seen in Chapter 2, is a more-or-less sophisticated or complex account of how or why aspects of the social world are as they are. Durkheim, as we saw above, had a fairly sophisticated theory to account for suicide. Although Durkheim gathered suicide statistics and examined them, his study did not, as we have suggested, actually start from the empirical data. He already had some notions about the causes of suicide. Indeed, he had a clear ontological starting point – that people are social beings and external factors impinge on the life and actions of individuals. Furthermore, his study of suicide was based on an epistemological presupposition that it is possible to establish the causes of social phenomena, in this case the causes of suicide. Durkheim's preconceptions about the transition from traditional to modern societies also gave him some hunches about the causes of suicide. He examined the statistics in an attempt to refine the vague theory he was developing.

Durkheim needed evidence (provided by suicide statistics) not only to make his theory convincing but also to help him develop the theory. This he did by testing out a series of *hypotheses*. These are simple statements that deal with a small part of the theory. For example, Durkheim thought that religion might be a factor affecting the extent of suicide. So, in effect, he set up the following hypothesis: different religious groups have different rates of suicide.

OPERATIONALISING CONCEPTS

Positivistic sociology, in its attempt to determine causal relations, needs to 'measure' factors so that they can be compared, for example the rate of suicide amongst one religious group compared to that amongst another. To be amenable to measurement, theoretical concepts need to be defined in terms of identifiable 'things', such as observations, statements of opinion or historical data. This is known as 'operationalising' concepts. In Durkheim's hypothesis, above, we would need to operationalise the concept of 'religious group' and 'suicide'. What constitutes a religious group? Which religious groups are included in the analysis? How do we define whether a death is a suicide or not? All these points have to be clarified so that we can actually measure suicide rates among different groups.

Durkheim noticed that suicide rates were higher for Protestants than for Catholics or Jewish people. Durkheim's main analysis compared rates of suicide between Protestants and Catholics. Suicide rates relate to different countries, not different religious groups, so Durkheim had to make comparisons, for example, by comparing countries that were predominantly Catholic with those that were mainly Protestant. Durkheim was relying on existing suicide statistics; he was in no position to collect his own first-hand data. He was thus restricted to the definitions of suicide that are used when deaths are officially classified as suicide.

When a concept is 'operationalised', that is, it is specified in a way that allows you to measure it, then it is known as a 'variable'. It is called a variable because it varies. A variable must have at least two 'values'. So in Durkheim's study, 'religion' as a concept becomes operationalised as 'religious denomination' which has values such as 'Protestant', 'Catholic', 'Jewish' and so on. 'Suicide' as a concept becomes operationalised as 'official suicide' and has just two values – 'death designated as suicide', 'death not designated as suicide'.

Activity
Suppose you have been commissioned to test the theory that there is a relationship between social class and educational achievement. In small groups, identify the dependent and the independent variables. Operationalise the concepts of 'class' and 'educational achievement'. When you have finished compare your operationalisation with other groups in your class. Make a list of other relevant independent variables that might affect educational achievement.

DATA COLLECTION

The key to data collection for positivist sociologists is to obtain data that can be used to check the hypothesis. Ideally, this data should not be biased but should give a 'fair' chance of the hypothesis being rejected or accepted. In that sense, the data used in hypothesis testing must meet similar criteria to the natural scientific experiment. The problem, for positivist sociologists, is that it is not possible to control the social environment in the same way that a natural scientist can apparently control the laboratory environment.

Furthermore, a positivist sociologist is not always able to 'observe' or obtain information about the 'perfect' setting that would enable a 'fair' test of a hypothesis. Either the data cannot be obtained or it is biased in some way.

Durkheim, for example, wanted data on the suicide rates of religious groups but had to settle for national suicide rates and compare the rates in Catholic countries with those in Protestant countries.

Bias in data occurs when it does not 'represent' the population that it is intended to represent. For example, if data on suicide rates in a country only related to those people who live in cities (perhaps because it is too difficult to collect data from outlying country areas), then the data would be biased as it would not represent the whole country. In most cases, the question of representativeness arises when a sample of people is used to provide information about a whole population.

For example, opinion polls do not ask everyone in the country who they would vote for at the next general election. Instead only a relatively small sample of about 1,000 people are questioned. If the sample has an appropriate proportion of males and females, ethnic groups, people from different socio-economic backgrounds (reflecting the population as a whole) and is spread across the country, then the result of the survey will be very close to the result that would have been obtained from the entire population. It is said to be a 'representative' sample. If, on the other hand, most of the sample had consisted of people living in London, then it would not be a representative sample of the country and the result would be biased towards views of people living in the capital. Equally, if no women had agreed to answer the questions, the sample would be biased towards males and again would not be representative of the intended population. There would, in this case, be what is known as 'non-response bias'.

(Note that a 'population' does not necessarily mean the population of a whole country. If you were investigating the views of patients in a particular hospital, for example, the 'population' would be all the patients in the hospital on a specific date).

Positivist sociologists look for four things from data used to test hypotheses:

1 Validity – does the data being collected actually measure the concept being investigated? (For example, does Durkheim's use of national suicide rates measure the extent of suicide in different religious communities?)
2 Reliability – is the data being collected in the same way each time? (For example, did all the countries examined by Durkheim compile suicide rates in the same way?)
3 Accuracy – is the data recorded accurately, that is, without making mistakes? (Durkheim, of course, could not have known if the clerks of the day had made any mistakes in compiling the figures.)
4 Representativeness – does the data represent the 'population' it is supposed to represent? Are the proportions of the different categories of people in the sample similar to the proportions of these different categories in the population that is being explored? (For example, in Durkheim's case, the data was for entire countries so there was no question of whether the data was a representative sample. On the other hand, were the statistics for the years he examined representative of the suicide rates in other years?)

Reliability and validity, it should be noted, are quite distinct features of data collection. It is, for example, possible to obtain the same or very similar results time and time again yet still fail to measure that which was intended to be measured.

Positivist sociologists use a variety of methods to collect data (see Chapter 2). These include the use of already – collected statistics (such as the official statistics used by Durkheim), social surveys (in which a representative sample of respondents are asked the same questions), analysis of documents or records, systematic observation, or even controlled experimental situations (such as the use of one-way mirrors to observe groups of experimental subjects).

In most cases, although not all, positivist sociologists try to end up with some form of quantitative data so that they compare numbers in different categories. To develop a causal analysis, Durkheim compared the rate of suicide amongst Protestants with the rates amongst Catholics and other religious groups.

Although, in theory, the hypothesis precedes the data collection, in practice, the hypothesis has often to be amended to fit the reality of the data available, or the limitation on what it is possible to collect. So, in effect, Durkheim's hypothesis had to be changed to: Protestant countries have higher suicide rates than Catholic countries. He then, in effect, had to 'operationalise' this by defining what constituted 'a Catholic country' and 'a Protestant country'.

MULTIVARIATE ANALYSIS

Multivariate analysis sounds complicated and many novice sociologists are put off by the concept because they think it is about the use of complicated statistical procedures. To the contrary, multivariate analysis is the basis of the analytical process used by positivist sociologists. It translates the principle of falsificationism into practice in a social setting.

The principle is straightforward. A hypothesis is set up that asserts that one variable is dependent on another variable. For example, the rate of suicide is dependent on religion. There is a 'dependent' variable (suicide) and an 'independent' variable ('religion'). Being clear which is dependent and which is independent is important as it shows the direction of the expected causal link. Suicide depends on religion, religion does not depend on suicide (it would be too late by then!).

The data that is collected is used to test out the relationship between the two variables (this is known as a 'bivariate' relationship). Durkheim's data, for example, showed that the suicide rate in Germany (a Protestant country) was higher than in Italy (a Catholic country). Similarly, he could have shown that the average suicide rate in all Protestant countries is higher than the average suicide rate in all Catholic countries. This would suggest that the 'bivariate' relationship 'suicide depends on religion' is correct.

However, to be a 'fair test', we need to take account of other factors that may distort the findings. It may be that it is nationality, not religion, that affects the rate of suicide. Nationality would be a third variable, it would be another 'independent' variable in this case. Durkheim tested out the possibility that nationality affected suicide rates by comparing the rates in the Catholic areas of Germany with the rates for the Protestant areas and showed that the Catholic rates were still lower. So, it seems likely that nationality is not important.

What has happened here is that the bivariate relationship between 'suicide' and 'religion' has been elaborated by using another variable 'nationality'. Nationality was used to see if the relationship between suicide and religion would disappear, or, as it is known in multivariate terms, to test whether the suicide–religion relationship was 'spurious'.

The independent variable 'nationality' is known as a 'control' variable as it controls the setting in which the suicide rates are compared, in this case, to just one country. The data showed that the suicide–religion relationship was not spurious when controlling for nationality.

The principle of multivariate analysis, then, is as follows:

- Specify a relationship between X (dependent variable) and Y (independent variable).
- Collect data to see if X is related to Y.
- If so, test to see if the relationship between X and Y is spurious by testing for one or more other independent control variables, to see if the original relationship between X and Y disappears.

- If it does, the original relationship is 'spurious'. If it does not, then we have more confidence that the relationship is 'real' and can be used to develop a theory.
- So, in essence, multivariate analysis moves the theory forward by attempting to disprove relationships.

The process defined here is the basic principle of multivariate analysis. The approach can, and often is, made more complicated by attempting to build and test out complex causal models.

Another stage of multivariate analysis is to 'specify' the relationship. *Specification* can take two forms. First, showing how a non-spurious relationship can vary in different circumstances. For example, Durkheim's analysis showed that irrespective of religion, suicide rates were higher in cities than in villages. Second, develop the model to show how more than one independent variable relates to the dependent variable. For example, Durkheim showed that being married and having children also affected the rate of suicide.

Sampling error

The real complication, even for a simple analysis, is that the positivist sociologist is usually dealing with samples. Even if the sample is not biased, the sample data will not exactly match the population data. There will be some variation.

For example, if you toss a coin 20 times you would expect that it comes up as 'heads' on 10 occasions, assuming it is an unbiased coin. However, it will not be heads exactly 10 out of 20 times in practice, it will vary, mostly somewhere between 8 or 12 times. It is extremely unlikely, although possible, that if you tossed it 20 times they would all be heads (in fact this is likely to occur only once in 1,000,000 sets of tosses).

So although a representative (thus, non-biased) sample will closely reflect the population, it will not necessarily be identical, nor on the other hand is it likely that it will be very different. So any sample will have, what is known as 'sampling error'. This is not 'bias' but the variation due to choosing a sample rather than including the whole population. This is where statistical procedures tend to come in to the analysis. They are used to distinguish between a 'real' difference in results and one that could have resulted from 'sampling error'.

For example, if we have a hypothesis that says 'Jill is better at getting heads than Jack' and we had a sample data that showed Jill getting 11 heads from 20 tosses and Jack getting 9, would we say that Jill is better? No, we would not. The evidence is not conclusive because we would expect that degree of variation. There is a high degree of probability that in tossing a coin 20 times anyone would get 9 or 11 heads. In short, the difference is not big enough to be convincing. Statistical analyses help us determine what constitutes what is known as a 'significant' difference, that is, one that leads us to think there is a real difference, not just a variation due to taking a sample.

Multivariate analysis can become quite complex when developing complex models using 'advanced' statistical procedures, the meaning and rationale of which are sometimes difficult to grasp. However, modern computing now means that there is no longer a problem in having to spend considerable time computing statistics; much more important is to understand the purpose and limitations of statistical procedures, principles of multivariate analysis and of sampling error as opposed to bias.

GENERALISING RESULTS AND DEVELOPING THEORY

Finally, positivistic sociologists attempt to generalise from the results of their enquiries. They need to be able to suggest that the theoretical relationships they have discovered in their sample are applicable to a wider range of circumstances. If they cannot make a convincing case about the representativeness or wider applicability of their analysis then they are unable to suggest that modifications be made to theory, or that they have further confirmed a theory.

Positivist sociologists often undertake large-scale surveys so that they have large amounts of data that appear to be convincing enough to enable them to make generalisations about the whole population on the basis of their findings. After all, the aim is to find 'universal laws' (usually in inductive studies) or at least to propose theories that are widely applicable (in deductivist studies).

Furthermore, analysing the data (multivariate analysis) and generalising the results are not the end of the process. This has to be linked back to theory. This is not a mechanical process and requires further conceptual thought. For example, Durkheim's analysis showed how marriage and children as well as religion related to suicide. His theorising, however, involved a conceptual leap not directly provided by the data. His notion, for example, of egoistic suicide being caused by a lack of integration into society was a conceptual leap from the data that showed that Protestantism (a more individualistic religion) and a lack of family were linked to suicide.

MIDDLE-RANGE THEORISING

Robert Merton (1968) referred to this approach as 'middle-range theorising' to distinguish the approach from grand theoretical speculation on the one hand and microscopic analysis of specific activities on the other.

In essence, the positivist approach tends to be portrayed as methodical, with a clear sequence of activities. The sequence is 'circular' in that it starts with theory and ends with theory. However, Merton argues that it is more akin to a spiral than a circle, as each time round the theory gets more refined or becomes stronger by not being refuted. This process, as we have seen, is also closely linked to falsificationism: setting up an hypothesis (a conjecture) and seeing whether it is refuted. Using multivariate analysis this amounts to testing to see whether an observed relationship can be shown to be spurious when other control variables are introduced.

In practice, as we have suggested, the positivistic approach does not operate in quite such clear-cut stages as the model suggests. Sometimes hypotheses are constructed or 'reconstructed' after the data has been collected. The operationalisation process that should precede data collection, is often redefined once the range of available data is known. It is rare that a sample is really representative and, in practice, available data has to be used. Thus a justification has to be made that the data does not seem to be unrepresentative, otherwise no generalisations can be made and the theory is not advanced. In short, the neat models and prescriptions elaborated in text books about how to do research can virtually never be reproduced in the 'real world'. Indeed, it is rarely desirable that they are, as they would take away the flexibility of the researcher to respond imaginatively to changing circumstances and new insights.

EXAMPLES OF MIDDLE-RANGE THEORISING

Testing for spuriousness: incomes of art and design graduates
A survey of nearly 2,000 art and design graduates (Blackwell and Harvey, 1999) showed, amongst other things, that females earned significantly less than males even up to four years after graduation. Art and design is an area in which about two-thirds of graduates are female. However, taking the average income of all male and all female art and design graduates showed that females earned significantly less than males. That is, the difference was not likely to be accounted for by sampling error.

Could this difference be accounted for by other things? Several other factors, apart from gender, appeared to account for differences in income. First, the longer it is since graduation the more the graduate is likely to earn. The study covered graduates from 1993 through to 1996. Those who graduated in 1993, on average, had higher incomes than those who graduated in 1996. However, when the year of graduation was used as a control variable, female graduates still had lower overall incomes than male graduates.

Similarly, art and design covers a wide range of subject areas and there are significant differences in income within each area. Fine art graduates, for example, earn less than fashion and textile graduates who, themselves, earn less than product design graduates. Fashion and textiles tends to be a predominately female area and industrial design a predominately male area. So perhaps this could account for the difference in incomes. However, when the discipline was used as a control, the differences in male and female income did not disappear.

Other variables, such as age, social class, ethnicity, degree classification were also evaluated to see if they had any impact on income. Although age had some minor effect, the key variables were year of graduation and subject discipline. When these two variables were both used as controls simultaneously the relationship between income and gender remained (Table 3.2). Thus the researchers concluded that there is a clear gender bias in graduate income in favour of males in art and design.

	1993		1994		1995		1996	
Subject area	Male	Female	Male	Female	Male	Female	Male	Female
3-D design	17960	15260	13540	199230	12500	11800	10000	8800
Fashion and textiles		13620	10000	*13500*	14170	11990	11670	11060
Fine art	8990	*11000*	8850	*9480*	10060	8510	9010	8490
Graphic design, visual, commercial	19240	15890	18750	14670	15390	14750	12960	12180
Photography, film, television	13500	11000	17500	13970	13960	12780	12500	9790
Product, industrial, furniture design	20000	13750	20630	16250	15750	10830	12500	9170
Interior design	15000	*19500*	23750	20500	16670	15740	18220	14170
Other	20000	11140	21670	13030	16790	11810	13750	9420
All	**15460**	**13300**	**16400**	**12540**	**13870**	**11700**	**11990**	**10080**

Table 3.2: *Estimated mean income for male and female graduates by year of graduation and main subject area*

Italicised bold cells are those where females have higher average salaries than males.
(SOURCE: BLACKWELL AND HARVEY, 1999)

Activity

Is using average income an appropriate way of showing that females have lower incomes than males?

In which areas do female graduates have higher incomes on average than males?

Does this information falsify the hypothesis that female art and design graduates have the same incomes than male graduates? Or does it 'specify' the relationship and, if so, how?

Evaluating the evidence: race and sentencing

Roger Hood (1992) undertook a study to explore whether or not the larger proportion of ethnic minority respondents in custody was a result of biased sentencing or proportionately more involvement by ethnic minorities in activity that would lead to a prison sentence. Ideally, Hood argued the appropriate method to explore whether there was any racial bias in sentencing would be to follow a large cohort of cases from arrest through to final outcome (known as the 'disposition') in the Crown Court. However, there were insufficient resources for this so he decided to 'work backwards' from the Crown Court records. He compared the charges and dispositions of all ethnic minority defendants in a sample of West Midlands courts with a large sample of white respondents at the same courts.

To be a meaningful analysis, a range of other variables, that have a bearing on sentencing, had to be used as control variables. These independent control variables include the seriousness of the crime, age, employment status, gender, whether the defendant had pleaded guilty and 'above all, the court centre to which they had been committed for trial and the judge before whom they appeared for sentence' (Hood, 1992, p 184). In all, 15 legally relevant variables were included in the analysis.

Hood concludes that taking all the male cases across the West Midlands, that 'a black offender had a probability of receiving a custodial sentence about 5 to 8 per cent higher than a white offender. Asians, on the other hand, had about a 4 per cent lower probability'. He goes on to comment that, given the number of cases 'these differences were sufficiently large to be to the disadvantage of a considerable number of black defendants'. However, he asks 'Does this amount to evidence of discrimination?' (Hood, 1992, p 184).

Hood admits that no study can control for all the possible variables that might have an impact on sentencing in courts. However, the results were consistent, the relationship between 'race' and 'sentencing' was not spurious. The results showed a small but significant correlation between race and sentence. Nonetheless, Hood reminds us that 'it is, of course, always hazardous to move from correlation to explanation'. A correlation just shows that two sets of data are related; as one changes, in this case ethnicity, the other changes, in this case the percentage of offenders getting a prison sentence. However, that in itself does not mean a causal link. Any causal relationship can only be determined by the researcher, who, on theoretical grounds, uses the association between the data to infer a causal relationship.

Hood discusses his data in some detail, specifying the relationship (that is, showing how the relationship varies in different circumstances). For example:

> *There was strong evidence to suggest that factors which would have been regarded as mitigating the seriousness of the case if the defendant was white were not given the same weight if the defendant was black in the cases dealt with at Dudley courts. Yet they were given a similar weight for black offenders dealt with at Birmingham (Hood, 1992, p 186).*

He goes on to 'test' whether this might be a spurious relationship by asking whether black offenders sentenced at Dudley courts could have been less well served by the pleas of mitigation than those at Birmingham. Unfortunately, there is no way of measuring the performance of barristers and probation officers, but for a number of reasons, which he listed, Hood argues that this seems an implausible explanation. He does not directly test whether this relationship is spurious or not but rather undermines the plausibility of any theory that the barristers performed worse in Dudley than in Birmingham.

Taking the above, and much more evidence of a similar nature into account, Hood concludes that:

> *When one contrasts the overall treatment meted out to black Afro-Caribbean males one is left wondering whether it is not a result of different racial stereotypes operating on the perceptions of some judges. The greater involvement of black offenders in street crime and in the trade in cannabis, their higher rate of unemployment, their greater resistance to pressures to plead guilty, and possibly a perception of different, less deferential, demeanour in court may all appear more threatening. And, if not threatening, less worthy of mitigation of punishment. It was significant that being unemployed increased the risk of a black male getting a custodial sentence, but not, in general, for a white or Asian offender.*

Hood, in this conclusion, is 'theorising' beyond what the data directly 'tells him'. Indeed, he admits that 'this for the moment must remain speculation' but does suggest a clear case has been made for more research to explore the issue of race and sentencing in more detail. What he has done, in his conclusion, is to go beyond the analysis which shows different treatment for black offenders, to propose that this is unfair treatment and that it appears to be the result of racial discrimination. He speculates that this discrimination is based on the perception of judges. He does not just make this last bit up. The evidence shows that the variation in sentencing is different in different courts. Hence the reference to 'some judges' in his conclusion. Furthermore, Hood draws on other research that has suggested judges take demeanour and attitude into account when sentencing.

Retaining a falsified theory: the case of a neighbourhood watch scheme
A study was commissioned by the Home Office (Bennett, 1988) to evaluate neighbourhood watch schemes in London. The hypothesis of this study was that crime would be reduced as a result of neighbourhood watch schemes. For each

area in which a neighbourhood watch scheme was to be implemented, an area that was similar in socio-demographic terms, and which had no neighbourhood watch scheme, was selected for the purposes of comparison. The areas in which no scheme was to be implemented thus served the purpose of 'control groups', as in a scientific experiment. The crime rate was the *dependent variable* and the neighbourhood watch scheme was an *independent* variable that may have had an affect on the crime rate.

There are other possible independent variables, such as, the level of policing, the proportion of young people and the environment. However, by matching a neighbourhood watch area with a similar non-neighbourhood watch area it was hoped that the impact of these other variables would have been removed.

The study examined the rates of crime and residents' fear of crime in both areas one to two months before the implementation of the scheme in the experimental areas. In this way, an attempt was made to ensure that any changes that occurred in the experimental area can be shown to have taken place as a result of the implementation of the neighbourhood watch schemes as opposed to any other independent variable (although the matching process might have missed out some other important independent variables). Another survey was carried out 12 months after the implementation of the scheme.

The results of the study showed that crime had actually increased in the experimental areas (the areas with the neighbourhood watch schemes), although fear of crime had been reduced. In the 'control' areas (without the neighbourhood watch schemes), crime had either stayed the same or reduced. The hypothesis that crime rates would fall as a result of neighbourhood watch schemes was therefore falsified.

However, this did not lead Bennett to conclude that neighbourhood watch schemes were bad. As Williams and May (1996) pointed out, Bennett did not question the theory behind the implementation of neighbourhood watch schemes, nor did he think that the research design was poor. Instead Bennett argued that in the cases under study the schemes were poorly implemented '... the design of Neighbourhood Watch as expressed in the Metropolitan (London) police guidelines was not a good example of Neighbourhood Watch in general' (Williams and May, 1996, p 147). In this way the theory is saved from the apparent falsification.

Activity
Bennett's research attempts to follow scientific standards and it appears to be value-neutral regarding the implementation of neighbourhood watch. How far do you agree that this is the case? What do you think are the weaknesses associated with this type of research? Are there, for example, problems of validity in this study?

Using a non-typical sample to falsify a hypothesis: the affluent worker
Researchers who are following the falsificationist method do not always choose a representative sample. Sometimes they search for untypical cases. The most famous example of a falsificationist study using a *non-representative* sample is Lockwood and Goldthorpe's *Affluent Worker* study in which they attempted to falsify the theory that the affluent working class were adopting the lifestyles of the middle classes. This was called the *embourgeoisment thesis.* They chose a sample of the most affluent workers because they would have been the most likely to have adopted middle-class lifestyles.

Lockwood and Goldthorpe did not find that the affluent workers had adopted the lifestyle of the middle classes so on this basis they were happy to reject the embourgeoisment thesis. Of course other theorists are free to test the hypothesis in different circumstances despite the falsification.

SUMMARY

The key point to remember is that the term positivism is associated with the view that sociology can be carried out in the same way as natural science. Its main purpose is to reveal cause-and-effect relationships. This means that positivist sociologists conceptualise society in the same way as natural scientists would conceptualise the natural world. Just as the natural world cannot be said to have thoughts and feelings, positivist sociologists choose to treat the social world in a way that, in general, ignores the thoughts and feelings of the individuals that make up society.

In sociology, the term positivism is used to refer to both inductive and deductive reasoning.

Induction assumes that:

- researchers can rid themselves of all preconceptions;
- data precedes theories;
- 'facts' can then be collected through careful recording of observations;
- a series of observation statements can lead to universal statements or 'laws'.

Deduction assumes that:
- theories precede data, that is, 'facts' are derived from theories;
- universal laws cannot be found;
- sense experience is not a sound basis of scientific knowledge.

In practice, falsificationism is the deductivist approach adopted in social science. It requires that:

- researchers should subject themselves to critique by forming falsifiable hypotheses;
- theories that remain unfalsified are the best we can have for now.

In reality science operates both inductively and deductively, as Durkheim's study *Suicide* illustrates.

Science is carried out within particular frameworks or paradigms, which tend to remain unquestioned until there are many puzzles that cannot be solved.

Despite these disagreements about the precise nature of 'the scientific method', most positivist sociologists agree with the following basis elements of the positivistic approach:

- review existing theory and establish a hypothesis;
- operationalise concepts;
- collect data;
- test the hypothesis using multivariate analysis;
- generalise from the results and suggest changes to theory and propose new hypotheses to test.

Positivist sociologists look for four things from data used to test hypotheses:

1 Validity – does the data being collected actually measure the concept being investigated?
2 Reliability – is the data being collected in the same way each time?
3 Accuracy – is the data recorded accurately, that is, without making mistakes?
4 Representativeness – does the data represent the 'population' it is supposed to represent? Are the proportions of the different categories of people in the sample similar to the proportions of these different categories in the population that is being explored?

Sociologists within the positivist tradition also argue that researchers should not become involved in making suggestions as to the way the world ought to be, rather they are in the business of explaining what the social world is like.

As the previous chapter indicated, sociologists do not agree on whether or not it is possible to separate facts and values in the way that positivistic sociologists suggest. The research examples that we have examined suggest that, in practice, the fact-value separation is more imagined than real.

Positivist sociologists use a wide variety of methods of data collection including observation studies, in-depth interviewing and content analysis. However, they often carry out large-scale studies using questionnaires or structured interviews.

Group Work

Task:

Design a positivist study to look at the number of people out of work in the north-east of England and the reasons for their unemployment. Identify the theories that you might use to explain unemployment. Identify a hypothesis about the causes of unemployment. Outline the methods that you would use and why they are appropriate. Each group should present their proposals and the similarities and differences in approach should then be discussed.

Practice Questions

1 What is meant by the terms deduction and induction? Does falsificationism resolve the differences?
2 Do you think that statistical data is value-free? Critically discuss your answer.
3 Evaluate the claims made by positivists that sociology is and should continue to be a 'scientific' discipline.

4

PHENOMENOLOGICAL SOCIOLOGY

THINKING PHENOMENOLOGICALLY

PHENOMENOLOGY IS ANOTHER way of knowing and describing the social world. This chapter outlines the key perspectives that can be placed under the broad heading of phenomenology. Phenomenology assumes that the study of the social world is fundamentally different to the study of the natural world. This is because the social world is made up of acting, thinking subjects whose actions require interpretation.

Phenomenology incorporates a diverse range of ideas but, in the main, the focus is on meaning and interpretation. In this approach to sociology the key purpose is to interpret people's actions rather than to explain them. For that reason, phenomenological approaches are sometimes referred to as 'action' approaches.

Phenomenological sociologists have rejected the idea that external truths about the social world can be exposed by using the methods of the natural sciences. They argue that people are not 'things', on the contrary people are conscious and purposive actors. Thus, phenomenologists argue that it is wholly inappropriate to treat people as if their actions are mere reflexes of external causes. So, although it might be possible to analyse the world of inanimate objects in terms of cause and effect, phenomenologists argue that how people behave is dependent on their conscious reflection.

We can sum up the phenomenological approach in the following fashion:

- individuals have ideas about the world in which they live;
- they attach meaning to social events, institutions and actions;
- they act on the basis of these ideas and meanings.

This approach requires that researchers should ask questions about the beliefs that people hold and the meanings that they attach to action. Researchers need to be concerned with the inner world of their subjects to be able to understand why people act in the ways that they do. The process of ascertaining the meanings which people give to their actions is called 'agency'.

As we saw in Chapter 3, interpretation is not considered to be a concern of science, therefore, the emphasis on interpretation in phenomenological approaches can be identified as a major difference between positivism and phenomenology.

Table 4.1: *Key concepts (theorists) and questions in this chapter*	
KEY CONCEPTS	KEY QUESTIONS
Interpretation	Should interpretation be part of the process of social research?
Meaning	How do social actors understand their world?
Interaction	How do people adjust their actions in relation to others?
Verstehen (Weber)	Why does this concept challenge the language of science?
'Ideal types'	How did Weber use 'ideal types' in his research?
Social action (Schutz)	How did Schutz's understanding of social action differ from Weber's?
Subjective interpretations (Simmel)	How do individuals create and recreate society?
The self (Mead)	What elements make up the self?
Social construction	How are the same things constructed in different ways at different times and places?
Impression management (Goffman)	How do we modify our actions in the processes of interaction?
Indexicality (Garfinkel)	How do we make sense of things in specific contexts?
Structuration (Giddens)	How can structure be both constraining and enabling?

Study point

'Susan Hannaford's research on institutional establishments for physically disabled people found…that a wish to leave the institution was categorised as troublesome and inappropriate, and explained either in terms of a feature of the disability, such as 'multiple sclerosis euphoria' or in terms of a failure to accept disability' (Morris, 1993).

How might a phenomenological approach challenge the findings of Hannaford's research?

DEVELOPMENT OF PHENOMENOLOGICAL SOCIOLOGY

Phenomenological approaches to the social world are related to, but distinct from, phenomenology as a philosophical method. The latter involves the systematic investigation of consciousness. The key idea in *phenomenological sociology* is that people are conscious beings. This acknowledgement affects the way we need to explore the social world. If we accept that people are conscious and purposive social actors it is not logical to treat them in the same way as scientists would treat the inanimate and 'unconscious' objects of their studies.

The work of Edmund Husserl was particularly important to the development of phenomenological philosophy (Figure 4.1). He was keen to demonstrate the falsity of the assumed separation of scientific knowledge from people's everyday experiences and actions.

Husserl's philosophy is complex and multifaceted but a major element of his work was the idea that to interpret the meaning of a social phenomenon it is necessary to remove the layers of preconceptions that distort its essential meaning. This approach is known as transcendental phenomenology because it is necessary to transcend scientific explanations, prejudices, taken-for-granteds and 'common sense'. All of these conceal the 'essence' of a social phenomenon. Husserl argued for a process of 'bracketing' away prior conceptions (sometimes also referred to as 'reduction' or 'époché'). By 'bracketing' he meant setting to one side explanations based on specific ways of seeing the world. Husserl's first level of 'bracketing' was to set aside natural or positivistic scientific explanations, that is, to see a social phenomenon devoid of any so-called scientific explanation of its significance. The second level of 'bracketing' (or double reduction or double époché) is to set aside all one's own prejudgements, common sense or taken-for-granteds. Only then will you reach the essence of the social phenomenon.

One of the main problems that transcendental phenomenology presents for sociology is that it is not possible to establish the evidence for the process of reduction. The double reduction that reveals the essence is a personal process. The only way, for Husserl, of knowing when you have really got to the essence is that you just know. It becomes self-evident to you.

Craib (1992) has also pointed out that the sociological form of phenomenology omits experiences such as emotions, imagination and hallucination that were of interest to Husserl. However, this is not strictly true since feminist sociologists have pointed to the ways in which the language of science has excluded emotions as a topic for study (see, for example Harding, 1991). Since human beings do not separate thought from feeling in their everyday activities then a science of society that ignores the role of emotions excludes a significant aspect of social processes.

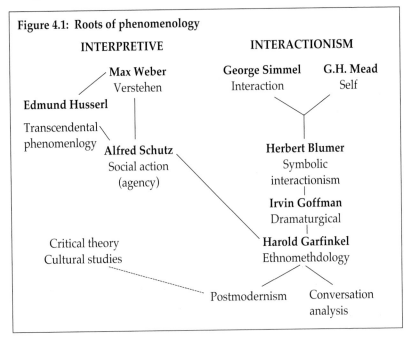

Figure 4.1: Roots of phenomenology

© Lee Harvey

Although phenomenology takes a variety of forms, we can identify two main strands, interpretive sociology and interactionism (Figure 4.1). The interpretive approach draws on the work of Weber ('Verstehen') and was subsequently developed by Alfred Schutz (social action) who was a pupil of Husserl.

The interactionist approach draws on the work of Simmel (interactionism) and Mead (symbolic interactionism). Building on the insights of symbolic interactionism Garfinkel (1967) developed ethnomethodology which in turn gave rise to conversational analysis and informed the development of postmodernism (Figure 1).

INTERPRETIVE APPROACH

Interpretive sociologists challenge the idea that we should treat the subjects of our studies as objects. Instead they focus upon the ways in which their subjects interpret or make sense of the world. Thus, in this approach, it is not for the researcher to decide in advance what the important issues are. Weber has been regarded as particularly important to the development of the interpretive approach although, as we shall see, he did not totally reject the concerns of positivism.

VERSTEHEN: WEBER

Weber objected to the positivist notion of objective, determining laws. He believed that such laws ignored the role of human action. Instead, Weber defined sociology as: 'a science concerning itself with interpretive understanding of social action and thereby with a causal explanation of its course and consequences' (Weber, 1978, p 4). In this way, Weber attempted to link cause with meaning. He referred to his approach as Verstehen.

Weber argues that there are two elements to the process of Verstehen. The first element relates to direct observational understanding (aktuelles Verstehen). For example, if you see someone typing at a keyboard you know what that person is doing but you do not necessarily know why. Sociologists must, according to Weber, also try to explain why something is happening (erklarendes Verstehen), that is, they should try to identify motives.

However, Weber was not just interested in individual motives; he was also concerned with social processes. Weber's method of doing this was to find a way of linking causes of action to the meanings people gave to their actions. Thus he distinguished between what he called 'meaning adequacy' and 'causal adequacy'.

Meaning adequacy relates to a plausible interpretation of action, given the context in which the action takes place. *Causal adequacy*, on the other hand, is when 'the relationships between the elements of a course of conduct can be shown to occur frequently, or preferably, invariably' (Waters, 1994).

For example, in *The Protestant Ethic and the Spirit of Capitalism*, Weber (1930) tried to show that ideas and beliefs influenced people's actions and that these actions influenced the development of capitalism. (As you will see in Chapter 5, this is the direct opposite of the analysis put forward by Marx.)

Ideal types

Weber challenged positivism in so far as he acknowledged the complexity of social life which, in turn, led to his rejection of direct observation as the key route to knowledge. Instead, Weber constructed *ideal types* of action to illustrate the different purposes behind actions.

He identified four different 'ideal types' of action:

1 Instrumental or goal-oriented action – action that has a clear aim;
2 Value-rational action – action that is influenced by a strong belief that something is right or important;
3 Affective action – action that is influenced by feelings such as love or hate;
4 Traditional action – action that has become a habit and is largely unquestioned.

Ideal types are not 'ideal' in the sense of perfect, or desirable, they are constructs that provide some insights into the process of gaining understanding. In effect, Weber was simply revealing the assumptions that he was making about types of action.

Use of ideal types in Weber's 'The Protestant Ethic and the Spirit of Capitalism'

In *The Protestant Ethic and the Spirit of Capitalism* Weber tried to show how the ideas behind the Protestant group known as Calvinists were important to the development of capitalism. The Calvinist religion encouraged people to work hard. At the same time Calvinists were also encouraged to live ascetic (or frugal) lives. This was because Calvinists believed in predestination, therefore they believed that only 'God' knew who were 'the saved' and who were 'the damned'. This belief led to a certain degree of insecurity which in turn led the Calvinists to look for signs that they were among the saved. It was reasoned by the Calvinists that the worthy would prosper but that also the worthy should not be wasteful or 'show off' their prosperity. According to Weber's ideal types the actions of Calvinists were *value-rational* actions. Weber noted the correlation between these value-rational actions of Calvinists and the development of capitalism.

This was 'the spirit' of capitalism because, according to Weber, it was this particular combination of ideas that enabled capitalism to take hold. Weber argued this because it was clear that, in order for capitalism to succeed, there had to be an accumulation of capital. If people spent everything without reinvesting money back into their businesses then their businesses would be more likely to fail. (In Chapter 5 you will see that Marx explains capital accumulation in a different way). Weber thus could claim that his analysis had *causal adequacy* as well as *meaning adequacy*.

In Weber's analysis value-rational action gave way to *instrumental* action because he theorised that in order to demonstrate that they were amongst the saved the Calvinists had to maximise their productivity.

Value-rational action can thus be seen to have had an unintentional consequence of producing a way of life (capitalism) that is characterised, above all, by an all-consuming instrumentality from which there can be no escape.

DISCUSSION OF WEBER'S METHODOLOGY

The emphasis Weber placed on the ideal type of goal-oriented action, tended to reduce the importance he placed on 'action' (as opposed to 'system').

It is almost as if Weber forgets that goal-oriented action is an ideal type or construct. He seems to end up assuming that goal-oriented action alone characterises modern capitalist societies. As Jones (1993, p.73) says so forcefully:

> ... *for Weber, Capitalism is the child of a particular way of thinking and acting, not a mode of production spawned by economic forces. But also for Weber this child should have been strangled at birth because it has grown into a monster.*

Although Weber was concerned to show the values that influenced people's actions, he also thought it possible, and indeed, desirable, to separate facts from values (see Chapter 2). However, Williams and May (1996) argue that the act of understanding must surely require us to make decisions between values.

So, although Weber wanted to reveal the values that had led to the development of capitalism, he did not wish to make any comment on those values, only to describe them.

Activity

Think about your own experiences of life. Do you think that people always act instrumentally in modern society? Provide reasons for your answer.

SOCIAL ACTION: SCHUTZ

The different elements of Weber's work revealed an ambiguity that was seized upon by later theorists. In particular, Schutz (1962) was keen to point out that any attempt to provide scientific explanations of people's behaviour would lead to the imposition of the researcher's views upon the individuals who were being studied.

Thus, Schutz argued that sociology should be about the ways in which people construct meanings. In his work on 'social action', Schutz further developed Weber's notion of Verstehen and more closely linked it to phenomenological philosophy. (Sometimes, Schutz's work is referred to as 'phenomenological sociology' because of this close link.) Schutz's work is fairly complex but in essence he shifts Weber's notions a little further away from positivism and places more emphasis on the conscious activity of the individual.

Schutz disagreed with what he regarded as Weber's assumption that the *meaning* of rational actions and *motives* for rational actions are essentially the same thing. Furthermore, Weber believed that instrumental action was the easiest form of action to interpret because it was rational. Schutz did not construe actions that were linked to emotions as irrational, or without meaning. Instead, he argues that the individual is able to think and operate according to a desired plan or strategy or 'project', as Schutz called it.

However, the individual is located in society and is thus a 'social actor'. Being a social actor means that the individual is constrained by social rules, norms or values. So when a social actor has a project in mind, Schutz argues that the project also takes into account the constraints that come from living in a society.

This, though, does not mean that the individual is constrained by external forces in the sense of causal laws proposed by positivists. On the contrary, Schutzian phenomenology proposes that people are seen as active agents who create and react to society rather than as 'puppets' who act in accordance with some external constraints. It assumes that individuals actively engage in interpreting, in terms of making sense of themselves, others and social and physical situations.

Schutz wants to take account of particular individuals making choices on the basis of their unique biographies and the specific features of the situations in which they do so. His primary concern with the ways in which individuals construct meaning is particularly strong in the sociological perspective called *ethnomethodology* – literally meaning people's methods (discussed below).

INTERACTIONISM

Interactionists are concerned to show that human beings are creative beings who can act purposefully. People do not simply act as isolated individuals, rather they act in relation to others. In deciding upon their actions, individuals take account of the ways in which they suppose that others will react to such actions.

SIMMEL

Georg Simmel was an influential sociologist at the turn of the century who was opposed to a positivistic approach to sociology. He was of the view that sociology should explore subjective interpretations rather than consider them outside the realms of a science of society. For Simmel, society is the sum of the interactions between individuals and as such, sociology should attempt to describe and interpret interactions.

In his book *Sociology*, Simmel (1908) attempted to answer the question, how is society possible? Unlike Durkheim (see Chapter 3) who saw individuals as socialised into society, Simmel argued that individuals have choices. This means that their integration is not inevitable, indeed, that individuals are never fully integrated but retain some individuality. Individuals do not just accept social norms and values they are, rather, active beings whose interaction creates and recreates society.

Simmel's study of the city *The Metropolis and Mental Life* attempted to demonstrate how city life changed people's behaviour. Early sociologists such as Durkheim were concerned about the changes that came about as a result of the change from traditional to modern societies. It is often assumed that modern society is characterised by selfish individualism and that people who live in cities are less caring than those who live in traditional or more intimate rural communities. Simmel tried to explain the interactions of people in cities in terms of the greater complexity of city life. People who live in cities only appear less caring because there is so much going on around them that they cannot take account of everything.

The impact on the development of interactionism attributed to Simmel rises and falls over time. His role was mainly forgotten through the 1960s and 1970s, especially when interactionism was linked closely to American sociology and seen to derive from the work of George Herbert Mead. However, later work has suggested that interactionism has rather more diverse roots (Harvey, 1987; Bulmer, 1984) and Simmel's role has been given more emphasis (Rock, 1979).

MEAD

George Herbert Mead was a social psychologist but his work is supposed to have been a significant influence on the development of interactionism. In practice, Mead, as we shall see, mainly influenced the strand of interactionism that later emerged as *symbolic interactionism* (see below).

The central concept for Mead is the 'self'. The self can be divided into two elements, the 'me' and the 'I'. The 'me' can be thought of as the objective self upon which the 'I' can reflect. For example, in your everyday lives you can probably think of many occasions when you have 'conversations' with yourself in the process of coming to decisions.

The self is constructed largely through language or symbols. Mead talked about the way in which young children learn to become social beings. In order to become social beings it is necessary to interact with others. The distinctive feature of being human is that we communicate through language. Communication can only be said to be truly taking place when both or all of the parties involved in the interaction understand each other. A good analogy might be if you are in a foreign country unable to speak the language. You could speak to another person in your own language but unless that person understands what you are saying

COMMUNICATION

you could not really be said to have interacted in any meaningful way. You might, however, resort to sign language or pictures to make yourself understood. When we act, we act in relation to others, that is, we try to understand their behaviour whilst at the same time modifying our own behaviour in relation to the ways in which people respond to us.

SYMBOLIC INTERACTIONISM: BLUMER

Blumer developed the work of Mead and produced a version of interactionism that came to be known as symbolic interactionism. Blumer (1969) summarised the principles of symbolic interaction as follows:

- Human beings act towards things on the basis of the meaning that things have for them.
- These meanings are the product of social interaction in human society.
- These meanings are modified and handled through an interpretive process that is used by each individual in dealing with the signs each encounters.

Blumer pointed out that when we interact with others we take certain things for granted. We do not create new meanings each time that we communicate with people. Thus, we can say that people construct meanings within a taken-for-granted framework that will usually remain unquestioned. However, people interact in a variety of circumstances. Therefore, they may, occasionally, find themselves in new situations that may cause them to adjust their meaning framework.

Activity
Think of a topic on which you have been persuaded to challenge your way of understanding an aspect of the social world, for example sexuality. How do new understandings of a topic affect subsequent interactions?

Hester and Eglin (1992) have demonstrated how Blumer's three key assumptions about interactionism can be applied to the study of crime. With regard to the first assumption, when we talk about crime we know that whether or not an act is constructed as criminal depends upon the meanings that we attribute to the act. Those meanings will vary in different societies and in different historical periods. For example, in Britain, marital rape was not considered a crime until 1992.

Reflecting Blumer's second assumption, the meanings we attach to specific acts are derived from our interactions with others. These interactions may also help us to stand back from our own actions. By taking the standpoint of others with whom we have interacted we are able to classify our own behaviour as either criminal or not.

Finally, our decisions as to what is or is not criminal will depend upon how the setting in which the act takes place is defined by the individuals who are party to it. For example, we know that it is against the law to kill someone but in the context of war we may not always construe the killing of another individual as a crime.

As Hester and Eglin (1992) point out, a Blumerian approach to crime would examine the processes of interaction through which:

- particular forms of behaviour come to be defined as illegal;
- particular people come to the attention of law enforcers;
- particular people are defined as criminal by the courts;
- a person's criminal identity is developed, maintained and transformed.

In the sociology of crime, the concern with the processes outlined above are linked to a particular strand of symbolic interactionism called the *labelling* perspective. Although labelling theorists, along with other interactionists, have been criticised for taking insufficient account of social structures, the questions asked by labelling theorists were very important because they shifted the focus of attention from those with least power to those who had the power to label others.

DRAMATURGICAL APPROACH: GOFFMAN

Probably the most well-known symbolic interactionist is Irvine Goffman, who likened social interactions to performances in a theatre. In the same way that actors play parts on the stage, Goffman says that we all play our parts in society and we act in response to our 'audience' (other people). Just like actors in a play, we put on a performance in public but, in private (or 'backstage') or with those with whom we are most intimate, we behave in different ways. In our everyday lives we choose which aspects of ourselves to reveal to others. We may choose to reveal different things to different people in different contexts.

If, for example, you are with a group of your friends you may use language that is acceptable to each other but which, perhaps, other members of society might find offensive. You would probably not use the same language if you were being interviewed for a job; you would want to create quite a different impression.

Goffman called these processes *impression management*. We can see that according to this approach there are not external 'rules' of society that manipulate our actions, rather our actions are constantly being modified in the processes of interaction. Symbolic interaction attempts to view human beings in relation to each other with the recognition that life is made up of complex processes of action and reaction. Human beings make sense of society by attributing meaning to facets of human life through these processes.

Goffman was also interested in the ways in which people may either intentionally or unintentionally discredit themselves. For example, you might walk into a job interview wearing your best clothes, feeling confident that you have the skills needed for the job and on your way you trip over a chair, fall to the floor and lose your confidence. Such incidents are beyond our control and may result in a 'spoiled identity' or in Goffman's terms, 'losing face'.

OVERVIEW

In more general terms, we can say that interactionists consider their job to be about providing formal descriptions of the micro social worlds that constitute a society, such as gangs, groups of people, pubs, families and schools. These are restricted social situations. They are created by people who experience them as sets of changing resources, opportunities, contexts and constraints. Shared symbols are used to define social situations. Some aspects of these worlds will be familiar and general and others will not be. The key to interactionists' approaches is not to presume how people make sense of their world before you have studied it. Interactionists argue that researchers can never know what they are exploring until it has been explored.

For example, Doris Ingrisch examined life history interviews in a study carried out for the Austrian Ministry of Women's Affairs and the Society of Ageing and

Culture in Vienna. This study focused on older women and the ways in which socially transmitted images of women's roles are related to age and identity. Ingrisch (1995, p 42) states that: ' ... the intention was to allow theoretical ideas to emerge through analysing and interpreting the women's accounts, rather than approaching the interviews with a particular theoretical orientation.'

Researchers in the interactionist tradition strive to keep an open mind on the social world, learning about it as they move through the research process.

Study point
In the light of the above information and information in Chapter 3 can you identify any points of similarity between interactionism and positivism?

ETHNOMETHODOLOGY

The ethnomethodological perspective is associated with the American sociologist Harold Garfinkel who aimed to reveal the ways in which people construct meanings for themselves in their everyday activities. Whereas symbolic interactionists focus upon shared meanings, ethnomethodologists focus upon the ways in which people arrive at those shared meanings, that is, they focus on process.

Ethnomethodology is concerned with detailed analysis of interaction on a small scale between individuals or within small groups. The focus of ethnomethodological analysis is on language, which is considered to be the fundamental resource for micro-social interaction. However, the concern is not the language in itself but what the use of language reveals about the shared understandings that actors have. That is, ethnomethodology is fundamentally concerned with taken-for-granted elements of social interaction.

Garfinkel (1967) involved his students in 'breaching' experiments in which the students were asked to breach the normal 'rules' of behaviour by asking 'what do you mean?' in response to straightforward questions, or act like guests in their own homes, or haggle for fixed price goods in shops. Garfinkel and his students discovered that people get rather angry with this sort of behaviour but nevertheless they also try to make sense of it. Imagine that you have just come out of an examination and you ask your friend 'how did it go?' to which you receive the reply 'how did what go'. You would probably feel irritated. If you then asked 'did you finish the paper?' and received the reply 'what do you mean, the paper?' your reflections on this reply might lead you to assume that your friend has 'really flipped', the stress of examinations has really got to them! This process of making sense of things in specific contexts is what Garfinkel refers to as 'indexicality'. The concepts of indexicality and essential reflexivity, the term Garfinkel used for these reflections, summarise the ethnomethodological view of language. They refer to the way in which the meanings of words depend on the context in which they are used and on their relationship to other words and events.

Maynard (1984) uses ethnomethodology to demonstrate the ways in which descriptions of defendants in court help to establish the justifications for the court recommendations. Maynard tape-recorded plea-bargaining sessions in American courts. Hester and Eglin (1992, p 220) state that Maynard's analysis demonstrates the following:

- both public defender and district attorney use defendant attributes such as sex, age, marital status, number of children, religiosity, occupational status and ethnicity, along with other features of the circumstances of the case, to determine what offence, if any, took place, and thus to justify proposed dispositions;
- the meaning of any attribute depends on its relationship to the collection of others;
- both these matters are assessed in terms of how the cases would look in court before a jury.

SUICIDE: THE SHIFT FROM INTERACTIONISM TO ETHNOMETHODOLOGY

In the previous chapter we used Durkheim's study of suicide as an exemplar of positivistic sociology. We are now going to briefly examine two other studies on the same topic, one that employs an interactionist approach (Douglas, 1967) and another that employs an ethnomethodological approach (Atkinson, 1977).

Douglas begins by questioning the 'facts' of suicide as given in the official statistics utilised by Durkheim. He assumes that the statistics are inaccurate. Rather than focusing on causal analysis, Douglas argues that it is more interesting to examine the meaning of deaths, described as suicide, to those who had taken their lives. To do this, it would be necessary to examine suicide notes and family reactions. In this way a more accurate figure of suicide may be established. Thus, Douglas focuses on the meaning of suicide to individuals.

Atkinson's study of suicide began in a positivistic fashion but during the course of his study his focus shifted, first from positivism to interactionism and second from interactionism to ethnomethodology. Atkinson's study differs from that of Douglas because his main focus ends up being on coroners' reports. The key question for Atkinson was how do deaths come to be constructed as suicide in the coroners' proceedings? Atkinson, unlike Douglas, makes no attempt to find a more accurate rate of suicide as he sees this as a useless and impossible task. It is not suicide that is of sociological importance to Atkinson, rather it is the way in which individuals make sense of particular circumstances surrounding such deaths. Atkinson, therefore, does not focus so much upon individual meanings but on social processes.

Study point

How do you think that an ethnomethodologist would approach official crime statistics?

CONVERSATIONAL ANALYSIS

Conversation analysis developed from the work of Garfinkel. The key theorist is Harvey Sacks who believes that the analysis of conversations is an ideal way of discerning the ways in which people construct meanings. Sacks attempted to set out the rules of conversation. In normal or everyday conversations people take turns to speak but there are occasions when the rules of conversation are formalised, such as in a wedding ceremony.

In police interrogations or counselling sessions, devices are used to encourage the other person to speak, for example a police officer could simply say 'Hmm' thereby indicating that the suspect is expected to say more.

However, the increasing focus on the structure of conversations in recent analyses can be said to have moved ethnomethodology away from its phenomenological roots.

POSTMODERNISM

Postmodernism is a term used to characterise a way of perceiving late twentieth-century culture. It has been developed, in particular, in relation to art, music, television and film. It has also been used as a tool for sociological analysis and it has been claimed as an alternative perspective on analysing the social world.

Postmodernism has a wide variety of 'roots' including linguistics and semiology, ethnomethodology, conversational analysis, psychoanalysis, Marxism (especially critical theory), structuralism and post-structuralism, hermeneutics, feminism, media analysis and film theory (see also Chapter 5). However, despite certain reasonably consistent elements, postmodernism is not a single approach and covers a variety of related perspectives. Further, postmodernism is somewhat predatory and the label of postmodernism has been retrospectively applied to approaches to sociology.

It might be argued that postmodernism is a critical (see Chapter 5) rather than a phenomenological approach to sociology. There is some superficial resemblance, which is discussed below, but in essence, postmodernism lacks the critical, dialectical approach of critical social research.

Postmodernism, despite a critical dimension, rapidly became dominated by an approach that attempted to reinterpret capitalism as a fragmented social structure in which rationality no longer provided a way of understanding the world. Theorists such as Michel Foucault (1977), Jaques Lacan (1968) and Jean-Francois Lyotard (1984) argued that capitalism provides a cultural context in which we live rather than a social structure that provides a set of constraints or rules that we must take into account, as Durkheim had proposed (see Chapter 3). This culture is not dependent on social structure but rather on ideology and social discourse and that people have considerable freedom of choice even within the ideological framework of capitalism.

As with other phenomenological perspectives, postmodernism has the following characteristics:

- it questions the positivist notion of causal science, especially its ability to determine universal truths independent of the interpretive process of individuals;
- it does not regard so-called scientific methods as value-neutral;
- it considers language to be an active medium for shaping our interpretation of the world, rather than a neutral process of representing the world.

In addition, postmodernism, in one form or another, develops further some aspects of phenomenology. Postmodernism:

- sees the 'self' as unstable rather than rational. Mead's notion of the self, for example, as tempering the different requirements of the 'I' and the socialised 'me' implies a self-reflective process that postmodernists consider unrepresentative of the individual in a fragmented and complex society;
- does not see knowledge as neutral and based on rational thought, instead it sees it as reflecting particular interests – this effectively restates Husserl's transcendental phenomenology which attacks the essence of scientific rationality;
- tends to see knowledge as 'relative' rather than 'absolute' and, as a result, is opposed to any type of grand theorising about the social world.

A principal approach of interpretive postmodernism is to 'deconstruct texts'. Deconstruction, in this sense, means 'to break down' texts in order to grasp the implicit meanings. These implicit meanings are grasped when the underlying assumptions in the text are exposed. A 'text' is 'any form of symbolic representation of meanings' such as writing, film or recorded speech. So, for example, Gregory Matoesian's (1993) analysis of the discussions and exchanges in American rape trials attempts to reveal underlying sexist attitudes in the prosecution and defence of rape cases. Reflecting the ethnomethodological influences on interpretive postmodernism Matiesian undertakes a conversational analysis of the exchanges in the courtroom, which he tape-recorded and transcribed in detail, including the pauses, hesitations and inflections on different words. He expected that a detailed analysis of the transcripts would help him expose underlying assumptions.

Arguably, postmodernist deconstruction approximates Husserl's first level of 'reduction' (or époché), that is, it sets aside 'scientific' preconceptions about what constitutes reality, evidence or truth. However, it rarely approaches the transcendental level of the 'double époché' to determine the essence of a text.

As we shall see in Chapter 5, deconstruction and reconstruction is an essential element of critical social research. It is tempting to see postmodern deconstruction as the same thing. However, critical deconstruction means taking things apart so as to discover how it is that they are as they are. Deconstruction, for interpretive postmodernism, is premised on the idea that we can not theorise about why? or how come? The social world is as it is, besides which the social world is so heterogeneous that theorising can only be superficial. Deconstruction, for the interpretive postmodernist, is more akin to mapping how discourses reveal inequalities and injustices.

Postmodernists often refer to 'discourses' but they use the term in two different ways. In one sense it refers to micro 'discourses', such as a conversation, and means much the same as 'text', as in Matoesian's study of courtrooms. In another sense, a discourse is a body of ideas, knowledge and beliefs. In that case, it is similar to a 'world view'. A 'discourse' can be seen as a way in which (dominant) culture is transmitted through religion, education, media and arts. It parallels, to some extent, the notion of 'culture'; a term to imply that there is a set of expectations expressed via speech, secular and religious teaching, media, literature and the arts that embody appropriate behaviour in a given social setting. For example, Foucault explored how madness became constructed as a discourse that changed over time as different conceptions based on religion and medicine became dominant. A discourse, in this sense, is not a 'theory' but a set of interrelated conceptualisations that not only attempt to account for madness but also affect the way in which people react to, and perceive, madness.

Postmodernism thus attempts to reinterpret the social system exposing injustices and inequalities that are embedded in discourses. What interpretive postmodernism is attempting to do is to question taken-for-granteds about the social world by showing how dominant 'discourses' are established and maintained.

There is, for example, one element of feminism, particularly that which draws on psychoanalysis, that sees itself as closely allied with the concerns of postmodernism (Kristeva, 1984). This can be seen in film theory. Feminist critics, for example, have used psychoanalytic processes to argue that the classic Hollywood films are made in such a way that the viewer is given the view of male onlooker rather than that of a female. Feminist film, they argue, needs to 'deconstruct' this dominant way of seeing (women) and provide a new cinema that abandons a dominant perspective altogether. In this way, instead of a male view being replaced by a female view the viewer would be able to actively interpret the film from an array of perspectives.

Postmodernism differs from critical social research in three ways. First, postmodernism is reluctant to develop theories. Second, it is apolitical, and acts as sceptic rather than critic. Postmodernism has been described as 'playing radical games with the system' but as being 'more a clever commentary on capitalism than an analysis of the system' (O'Donnell, 1993, p 522). Indeed, postmodernism has been criticised for not being critical in the sense of providing a fundamental critique of society. O'Donnell, for example, regards postmodernism's failure to critique the increasing concentration of wealth and power evident in the international capitalism as irresponsible. Third, postmodernist deconstruction does not lead to an alternative reconstruction (see Chapter 5).

EXAMPLES OF PHENOMENOLOGICAL SOCIOLOGY

Three examples, from different areas, will be used to illustrate the phenomenological approach.

PETTY CRIME

Dick Hobbs adopts a phenomenological approach in his study of petty criminals and the local CID in the East End of London. Hobbs argues that his research is about 'both formal and informal control strategies and the coercive regulatory power of the market place' (Hobbs, 1988, p 1). He studies the police using the perspective of the petty criminals who also formed part of his research. Hobbs situates his research within the context of the development of the British police and the CID and the economic history of the East End of London.

This research is an ethnographic study that utilised participant observation and in-depth interviewing. Hobbs gained access to his subjects in a variety of ways:

- from his local pub where CID officers also drank;
- from his role as football coach of a team where one of the parents was also a CID officer;

- from family and friends who were part of his life when he lived in the East End;
- from police officers who agreed to be interviewed formally in their homes about CID procedures.

Hobb's research led to him spending time in a variety of pubs drinking with his research subjects. Some writers have argued that Hobb's ethnographic study was enriched due to his own background as he was born and lived in the East End of London. Thus, we could argue that Hobbs as the researcher was very much an insider and that this made his access, both to the petty criminals and the police, easier as he shared the same knowledge of the area as his research subjects. However, his relationship with the petty criminals was more sympathetic and involved than the relationship with the police, which was more constrained. In part, this was due to the racism and sexism displayed by the police respondents, which Hobbs found difficult to accept. Thus the data from the police was not as detailed as that from the petty criminals.

During the course of the research Hobbs used both overt and covert participant observation. He overtly observed the situation when he visited CID offices and covertly observed informants at clubs, in the pub and at parties.

Hobbs acknowledges that crime is a considerable problem for the working class in inner city areas but at the same time argues that if attention is focused on 'intra-class' crime it will result in more emphasis on the control and containment of working-class crime. Rather, Hobbs argues that the way the CID operates in the East End of London is very different from the way it operates in other areas. This difference is because of the culture of the East End. This culture is characterised by features such as independence, masculinity, acceptance of 'deviant identities' and, importantly, 'an entrepreneurial ability', which the police themselves have adopted. Thus, Hobbs argues, the economic history of the East End of London has resulted in what he calls a 'trading culture', which is both accepting of petty crime and also affects the CID detectives' everyday practice. Hobbs then utilises this concept of 'trading culture' to analyse his informants' understandings of their lives.

MOTHERS AND THEIR DAUGHTERS-IN-LAW

Cotterill (1994) begins with the observation that there is very little positive imagery regarding the mother-in-law/son-in-law relationship. It is usually assumed that if conflict occurs it will be between the husband and his mother-in-law and not between the wife and her mother-in-law. Amongst the wealth of sociological studies on 'the' family there is very little data on in-law relationships between women, and feminist literature has focused primarily on relationships of power between men and women. Thus, methodologically, Cotterill began her study by identifying the gaps in existing literature.

Cotterill describes her study as one that 'explores how people's relationships are structured by their positions in the family network and how these relationships are supported and maintained within the context of private and public notions of family life' (Cotterill, 1994, p 2).

The study is based upon 106 interviews with a sample of 35 women, 10 mothers–in-law and 25 daughters-in-law. The participants were aged between 19 and 72, all were white. Twenty three of the women were middle class. The women were encouraged to 'tell the story' of their in-law relationships. This is in line with the general concern of phenomenology to 'tell it like it is'. As a result of these in-depth interviews key themes were developed. Thus, the life history approach was augmented by semi-structured interviews in which the women were encouraged to reflect upon specific themes and issues. Finally, the women were presented with vignettes (descriptions of hypothetical events or situations) so that information could be gained about commonly held norms. Cotterill notes that these vignettes often led the participants to reveal more intimate details of their own relationships without there being any pressure on them to do so.

The study points to the ambivalence of family within the social structure as a whole by focusing upon what Cotterill says is, arguably, the most ambivalent relationship within 'the' family. Just as older women are marginalised from society, so mothers-in-law are marginalised in family relationships. They are simultaneously both inside and outside 'the' family. The overall purpose of the study was to generate further debate by exploring the meanings that the participants gave to their experiences. It can be seen from this that there was no intention to make large, generalised statements. Rather the intention is to obtain authentic data that can be used by others in further studies.

RACISM

Benjamin Bowling's (1998) study of racism in Britain is focused on a case study of an area of London. The first part of the book sets the context for the case study. It describes the history of racism in Britain, the emergence of racism as a public issue and the formulation of government and police policy. Theoretical and methodological debates in criminology are also explored. However, this contextual information is not used as the basis for a critical social research study (see Chapter 5)[1], but rather provides a broad setting for the specific acts of racism explored in the study. Bowling concentrates on the meaning that racist events have for those who experience them and those who police them.

---

[1] A critical study would, for example, have related the empirical data back to the social and political context and used the data to deconstruct the nature of racism and build an alternative analysis of the role of policing within the production and reproduction of racism. Bowling does not do this.

The case study is the North Plaistow Racial Harassment Project set up to combat racism in an area of east London. The data collected consisted of two phases. The first was the 'problem description phase', which attempted to identify the nature and extent of racial harassment. The data for this phase came from three sources: police files, 23 group interviews and a victimisation survey that resulted in 751 individual interviews of which 169 respondents were from ethnic minorities.

The second part of the data collection was the 'evaluation phase'. This involved 'further analysis of recorded incidents, interviewing officers from the agencies involved, and observing them during their work'. The formal observation and interview sessions were also 'augmented with long periods of conversation with police officers of various ranks and from various specialisms' (Bowling, 1998, p. 172). In addition, Bowling collected further information from individuals connected with or affected by the project, including two detailed studies of victims of violent racism.

Much of the initial analysis includes illustrative quotes describing racial harassment but also includes some statistical material showing, for example, that the main perpetrators of racial harassment are males, between 16 and 25 acting in a group. What emerges from the accounts is that

> *the experience of violent racism is not reducible to an isolated incident, or even a collection of incidents. Victimization and racialization – the process by which a person* **becomes** *a victim of this form of crime – are cumulative, comprised of various encounters with racism, some of which may be physically violent, some lying at the fringes of what most people would define as violent or aggressive (Bowling, 1998, p 230)*

The response of the police to racial harassment and to violent racism is further explored through the observation process and the qualitative accounts of individuals in the survey who had reported racial incidents. As a result of the data collection, Bowling argues that 'while violent racism is a *social* process, the police and criminal justice system respond to *incidents* (Bowling, 1998, p 285). It is this contradiction between ongoing process and individualised incident that underlies the dissatisfaction of victims with police response, despite improvements in police policy. Policy and practice in relation to racial harassment and violence improved through the 1980s but reached a plateau at the end of the decade. In effect, racism remains a 'potent force' in the case study area and is regularly expressed in terms of violent acts. The result is that many families and individuals remain at risk of attack and live in fear of their safety. This is because the protection from the police is 'precarious' as it does not address the social process.

ELEMENTS OF THE PHENOMENOLOGICAL APPROACH

REVIEWING EXISTING THEORY AND IDENTIFYING GAPS

As in all research, phenomenologists are concerned to engage with the findings of research in related areas. Therefore, the research process begins with a review of the existing literature and the identification of gaps in existing knowledge. For example, as we saw, Cotterill (1994) chose to study the relationship between mothers and daughters-in-law as this is a topic which the sociology of the family had neglected. Power relationships between women had also largely been neglected by feminist studies on 'the' family.

Nina Eliasoph (1998) also identified a gap in sociological research. She found that there had been no attempt to study the sociological nature of apathy. Despite the importance of democracy, ordinary American citizens avoid appearing to care about politics. Thus Eliasoph attempted to explore how apathy was constructed as a public statement in the United States.

PROBING MEANINGS

Phenomenological research is particularly concerned to present the topic under study in the participants' terms. The meaning that a topic has for the participants is, therefore, far more important than the researcher's perspective. Bowling (1998), for example, found that despite increased policing in the area under study, black people's experiences revealed that they were still at risk from racist attacks.

Geoffrey Weeks *et al.*, (1996), in a study of non-heterosexual relationships, probed the meaning of 'family' for the non-heterosexual participants in their research. They conducted in-depth interviews with 48 men and 48 women who identified as non-heterosexual. The findings of this study suggested that although the term family is used to describe kinship groups with children, the non-heterosexual participants broadened the meaning to include significant friendships.

RECORDING DATA

Phenomenological research relies heavily on subjects' accounts, which may be derived from open responses to questionnaires, in-depth interviews, noted conversations, observations, and an array of different documents including letters, diaries and memoranda. As far as possible, phenomenologists attempt to record the statements and perceptions of the subjects accurately. This is frequently assisted by the use of technology such as audio tapes and video. Transcribing data for analytic use raises problems of codification and storage. At one extreme, as we have seen, conversation analysts attempt to specify every hesitation, emphasis and nuance.

The collection and recording of phenomenological accounts frequently leads to the generation of an enormous amount of detailed quotes, examples, anecdotes and so on. The production of a finished report requires a selection from this detail. The choice of material is guided by the theoretical framework (or angle) that has emerged during the study.

ANALYSIS

A major problem that phenomenological researchers face is how to deal with the vast amount of material. The data needs to be sorted, coded, organised and ultimately reported.

One widely used approach is 'horizontal and vertical' reading of the data. 'Vertical' reading involves reading the data chronologically from start to finish in order to become familiar with the content. As a result of this process, major themes that seem to recur throughout the data and have a bearing on the theoretical concerns, can be identified.

The data is then reread 'horizontally' by theme, and relationships between themes are identified. This process of horizontal and vertical reading suggests a number of organising concepts that help to make sense of the data. This is not a simple linear process, it is circular and usually on-going throughout the research. The overall purpose is to arrive at the interpretation that the subjects have and to identify shared themes.

CONCEPTUALISING THE INTERPRETATION

The analysis of phenomenological data takes a variety of forms (see, for example Ely *et al.*, 1997, Chapter 4) but at root the aim is to try and 'reveal' the interpretive frameworks of the subjects. Sometimes this is facilitated by using pre-existing interpretive frameworks, for example in his study of poor and stigmatised social groups, Simon Charlesworth (2000) recorded in-depth interviews and conversations. He interpreted them using the social philosophy of Pierre Bourdieu and Maurice Merleau-Ponty to reveal the social relations and experiences of a largely ignored social group.

Having grasped the subjects' interpretations these are formulated into conceptual frameworks. In phenomenological research it is often left to those who read the research to accept or reject the interpretive concepts proposed by the researcher.

There is also an issue as to who the audience is in the case of phenomenological research – the subjects of the research or the academic community? For example, William Foote Whyte's (1943) classic study 'Street Corner Society' was considered to be an exemplary analysis of the life of street gangs of the 1940s but was regarded with rather less enthusiasm by the subjects, especially the gang leader.

DUALITY OF STRUCTURE

Recent developments in sociology have led to perspectives that have attempted to overcome the dichotomies to which we have referred in Chapter 2, such as individual versus society, structure versus action. In particular, Giddens' structuration theory (1976) has influenced a variety of researchers who have tried to build bridges (May, 1997) between the polarised accounts of much sociological theorising. Whilst Giddens wishes to retain a sense of individuals as purposive actors, he accepts that phenomenological approaches have a tendency to neglect the material conditions in which people live their lives. There is also a tendency to neglect relationships of power, although the methods that are generally utilised by phenomenologists are likely to reveal the power imbalances in the experiences of different groups.

As we shall see in Chapter 5, much feminist theorising has attempted to utilise the insights of phenomenology whilst still retaining an interest in the material conditions within which women carry out their lives.

Giddens has set out his approach to sociology in a variety of texts. It is clearest in *New Rules of Sociological Method* (1967) and *The Constitution of Society* (1984). Giddens' approach can be summed up as follows:

- Society should not be treated as an external reality because society is created by the actions of its members.
- However, people cannot simply choose how to create society because they are born into a specific historical period, which is not of their own choosing (here the influence of Marx is discernible (see Chapter 5)).
- Structure can be said to have a dual capacity to constrain and enable human action. Giddens calls this *structuration*.
- Power is both constraining and enabling, since power can be used to challenge existing structures as well as to maintain the *status quo*.
- However, actions often have consequences that are unintended. It is these unintended consequences that produce structures because '... these may feed back to become the unacknowledged conditions of future acts' (Waters, 1994, p 49).
- Similar to Garfinkel and Goffman, Giddens also retains a focus on the way in which people make sense of the different situations in which they find themselves.

SUMMARY

- Weber, Mead and Simmel are all important to our discussion of phenomenology as they can be seen to be key contributors to the development of phenomenological sociology (or action perspectives in sociology). These perspectives include social action, interactionism, symbolic interactionism and ethnomethodology.
- Weber was concerned with understanding the motives behind people's actions. He called this process *Verstehen*.
- Weber's emphasis on Verstehen represented a shift from the epistemological concern with causal relationships in positivism to a concern with interpretation.
- In general terms, action theorists begin from the experiences of individuals rather than from the social structures within which people live. This approach assumes that individuals actively create the societies in which they live.
- The concern with interpreting action is different from the concerns of positivist sociologists who, as we have seen, do not think that interpretation is a concern of science.
- However, Weber did not break totally with the concerns of positivism because, in addition to his attempt to attach meaning to people's actions, he also attempted to find a causal explanation for their actions.

Phenomenological approaches focus on the inner subject world of the social actor rather than on society as an external entity. This means that phenomenologists have different ontological assumptions to positivists.

- According to phenomenologists, subjects actively create social reality in different times and places. Therefore, there is no reality that is beyond our consciousness of it.
- So, there is no point in assuming that we can treat the subject matter of sociology in the same way that natural scientists treat the objects of their studies. After all, people are not objects, we can think and feel and we can make decisions on the basis of these thoughts and feelings.
- This approach also emphasises the researcher as a subjective being because, to achieve an empathetic understanding, the researcher has to be able to identify with the world view of the group or person being researched. For example, in research on heroin users an ardent anti-drug campaigner would have problems identifying or understanding the meanings and intentions behind the drug taking. In Ingrisch's (1995, p 43) study, for example, '... an attempt is made both to give women a voice and to use the researcher's own experiences to interpret their meaning'.
- The epistemological and ontological assumptions of phenomenological sociology have implications for the methods of producing data. Phenomenologists prefer to talk to people, observe their interactions, or

analyse the conversations they have and the language they use.

- The methods used by phenomenological sociologists will produce 'rich', 'qualitative' data, which does not, on the whole, lend itself to enumeration, tabulation or statistical analysis.
- Phenomenologists assume that the focus on generalisation in positivistic studies results in a failure to grasp the rich details of people's lives through which it is possible to discern commonalities between different groups of people.

POINTS OF EVALUATION

- Just as positivistic approaches to sociology have been criticised for reducing human behaviour to the effects of social systems, so phenomenological approaches have been criticised for reducing social processes to states of human consciousness. Therefore, it is sometimes difficult to see how phenomenological approaches differ from social psychology.
- As we have already noted in Chapter 2, the tendency of theorists to polarise action and structure presents an oversimplified picture of social life. If you think about your own everyday experiences, you will realise that although there are many things that constrain our daily lives there are also many ways in which we are able to overcome those constraints. For example, you will be constrained by the times at which your school or college delivers your sociology course, but you can, to a certain extent, choose which institution to attend. You can also choose to work hard to get a good grade, or you can choose to do less work in order to spend more time on your leisure activities. Your decision will depend upon a variety of factors, such as what are your career aspirations? If you wish to go to university you are constrained by the fact that you will have to achieve specific grades but this does not mean that you are, in robot fashion, simply doing what 'the system' requires. Once at university, you may be constrained by financial pressures that result in the need to take time off from your studies to earn enough money to pay your bills and have a social life. If your parents are wealthy and willing to supplement your loan you will have an easier time than if your parents are not so wealthy and you have to work. These material differences are beyond any one individual's control.
- Giddens' theory of structuration attempts to overcome some of the difficulties that arise as a result of the polarisation of structure and action.

Group 1:

List the assumptions made by phenomenologists about the nature of science. Discuss how these assumptions affect their choice of methods.

Group 2:

List the assumptions made by phenomenologists about the nature of society. Discuss the extent to which you agree with these assumptions.

Practice Questions

1 On what basis do phenomenologists argue that positivist methods are inappropriate to the study of social life?

2 Critically discuss the phenomenological view that it is important to consider the meanings that social actors give to their actions when analysing the social world.

3 You have been asked to conduct some interviews about the experiences of young people and drug use. Discuss the type of interviewing that you would use and the approach that you would adopt, giving reasons for your choice.

5

CRITICAL SOCIAL RESEARCH

THINKING CRITICALLY

CRITICAL SOCIAL RESEARCH (CSR) is a term encompassing an approach to sociological enquiry that attempts to go beneath surface appearance. It attempts to do this by questioning the views of the social world that are usually taken for granted (Harvey and MacDonald, 1993).

This chapter examines how CSR provides an alternative to positivistic and phenomenological approaches. Where positivism seeks explanation, and phenomenology attempts interpretation, CSR aims for *understanding*.

For the critical social researcher, positivistic approaches are inadequate. The search for *explanatory* causes reduces the problem to component parts and takes them out of context. The explanation is limited to the interrelationship between the elements that have been identified as having an effect. It does not take into account the bigger picture in which this interaction takes place.

An analogy would be to suggest that you can understand how a car engine works by simply taking it apart, or that you can drive a car across London simply by having passed all the component parts of a driving test. For critical social researchers, understanding does not come from breaking social events or structures down into causally – related component parts. On the contrary, understanding comes from seeing things as a whole and placing social events in their wider social and political setting.

Similarly, critical social research regards attempts to *interpret* social interaction as also limited. Although interpretation provides some insights, it is often focused too narrowly on the process of interaction without taking the wider context into account. It would be like driving across London by focusing on each traffic hazard in turn without any map of where you are going.

CSR is informed by *critical* epistemology, a view that knowledge develops through critique and is constrained by history and structure. Sociological understanding thus involves more than determining causes or interpreting meanings. It requires locating events in a wider historical and social setting. For example, to understand a strike, it is necessary to do more than look for the causes of the strike or to explore the meanings of those on strike. It is necessary to relate the strike to the history of industrial relations, employment prospects, government policy, legal constraints, media campaigns and so on.

What is involved in critical social research is a process of *deconstructing* a dominant understanding and *reconstructing* an alternative understanding that reveals the underlying social and historical interrelationships.

In summary, critical approaches to the social world:

- attempt to dig beneath the surface appearances;
- locate social processes or phenomena in a wide social and historical context;
- acknowledges that values and politics impact on social theorising.

Table 5.1: *Key concepts and questions in this chapter*	
KEY CONCEPTS	KEY QUESTIONS
Dialectical analysis	How does dialectical analysis differ from attempts to find causes?
Critique	What is the difference between critique and criticism?
Structure and totality	How can interrelated social phenomena be shown to be a part of the historical social structures that precede them?
Abstraction	How do we abstract from reality?
Essence	What is the essential element of the social phenomenon being studied?
Praxis	Should social research be political?
Ideology	How do the interests of dominant groups come to appear 'natural'?
Deconstruction–reconstruction	How do varieties of evidence help us to challenge existing knowledge?
Semiology	What is the relationship between an image (or 'sign') and what the image means ('signifies')?
Marxism	How have different forms of Marxism informed critical social research?
Critical theory	How does critical theory differ from critical social research?
Anti-racism Feminism	How can critical social research uncover different forms of oppression?
Social criticism	To what extent does social criticism address the issue of ideology?

COMPARING APPROACHES

Let us briefly explore the differences between critical, positive and phenomeno-logical approaches to the social world. Let's take a concrete social phenomenon. Why is it that some graduates from university get the jobs they want and others do not?

A positivist approach would be to break the problem down by identifying the specific knowledge, skills and abilities ('attributes') that graduates need in order to get employed, taking into account (controlling for) the size of employer organisation and the sector of the labour market. On the basis of this, a set of preferred attributes might be determined by asking employers what they want. It would then be possible to predict the likelihood of a graduate obtaining the preferred employment. So, for example, some employers have a list of 'criteria' such as:

- a good class of degree in a numerate subject;
- ability to work in teams;
- evidence of leadership;
- experience of the world of work;
- good oral communication skills.

A phenomenologist would argue that such an approach might be indicative of the necessary attributes but is not sufficient to explain why some people get jobs and others do not. The problem, they would argue, is that it is not possible to provide generalisable explanations. The process of employing graduates involves people, each of whom have different ways of interpreting the recruitment process. The problem is that even if we could accurately identify the attributes of any given graduate, which would be unlikely as individuals have a complex array of attributes, it is not the *possession* of the attributes that will ensure success in getting a job but the *demonstration* of them during the recruitment process. This requires a close analysis of the interpretation placed upon the parts of the recruitment process by the recruiters and the applicant. How does the applicant convince the recruiters that he or she has what they want? The sociological enterprise, for the phenomenologist, is to explore the process of interpretation that is going on between recruiter and applicant as the former try and uncover whether the applicant would be suitable for the post and the applicant attempts to understand what is required and thus to represent themselves in the best light.

The critical social researcher would be mindful of the expressed desires of the employers and the specification of personal attributes required of applicants. Similarly, the critical social researcher would take into account the phenomenologist's analysis of how the specification is interpreted in recruitment processes. However, the critical social researcher would also want to set the recruitment process in a wider setting. The world of work is changing rapidly and so are the requirements of employers. On one hand, organisations are changing structure to accommodate new working practices, for example they are removing layers of management, they are tending to less hierarchy and more team project working. They tend to be reducing in size as certain types of workers (mostly manual labourers) are no longer being recruited. Increasingly, firms are contracting out parts of their work to smaller independent companies ('outsourcing', as it is known). All of this has an impact on the recruitment process, the type of graduate needed and the subsequent career of the graduate once recruited. Furthermore, large organisations are very diverse and the practices employed by the recruitment manager may not match with what the recruit's line manager wants nor what the company strategic manager may be looking for in the long run. Conversely, small organisations may not have the time, money nor skills to undertake elaborate recruitment processes and, even if they specify skills, they may abandon them in favour of recruitment of someone they know will 'fit in'.

In short, the critical social researcher wants to go beyond the skills' specification and the close analysis of the recruitment process to take account of the changing world of graduate recruitment to explore not what recruiters want nor what procedures they use but how they relate their practices to their needs in a rapidly changing, fiercely competitive, global market.

Study point

Sociological studies suggest that working-class children achieve fewer formal qualifications in school than middle-class and upper-class children. How do you think a critical social research approach would make sense of such research findings?

DEVELOPMENT OF CRITICAL SOCIOLOGY

Critical social research is not a new alternative to positivism and phenomenology. On the contrary, it derives from the very foundations of sociology. The dialectical analysis of Karl Marx is the earliest example of critical social research. (Dialectical analysis is a process of locating events or actions in a wider social and historical context and involves conceptually moving backwards and forwards between the specific part and the contextual whole. This is initially difficult to understand and is explained in more detail on pages 105–110) Critical social research is also found in the work of subsequent Marxists, feminists, anti-racists, black sociologists, structuralists, cultural theorists and post-colonialists (Harvey, 1990).

There is an enormous diversity within these areas and there is no attempt here to classify different forms of critical social research. Instead, a simplified 'map' of the development of critical social research is suggested and a few key critical social researchers are identified (Figure 5.1).

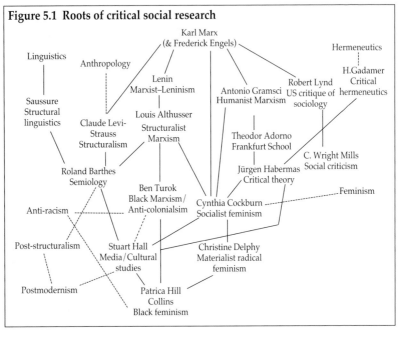

Figure 5.1 Roots of critical social research

© LEE HARVEY

Karl Marx is generally regarded as the first critical social researcher of the modern era. His work, throughout his life, critiqued the prevailing and dominant views of the world. He attacked taken-for-granted views about religion, social structure and, ultimately, capitalism. His work was not just an attack on the society of his day, rather it was an analysis of the way in which society operated to oppress the working class for the benefit of those with wealth and power. We look at an example of his work in more detail below. Marx, and his collaborator, Frederick Engels, were also concerned not just to analyse the world but to change it. Their analysis of capitalism, for example, was the basis for revolutionary political involvement and resulted in the *Communist Manifesto* (Marx and Engels, 1848).

Most subsequent work that has explored the nature of class oppression has drawn on the work of Karl Marx. In addition, a considerable amount of work on gender and race oppression has also drawn on the work of Marx and subsequent Marxists. Marx wrote extensively and there have been many different interpretations of his work, with different Marxists placing more or less emphasis on different parts of Marx's writings.

Two broad trends among Marxists have been identified: structuralist and humanist. As neat as this distinction is, it vastly oversimplifies Marx's work and the subsequent development of Marxism. Furthermore, when considering other branches of critical social research, notably those based on race and gender oppression, the distinction between humanist and structuralist approaches is not helpful. However, as many reviews of Marxism use this distinction we will adopt it below but it is important to remember that both humanist and structuralist concerns are found throughout the whole of Marx's work.

STRUCTURALIST MARXISM

Marxism is, therefore, varied and the debates that divide Marxists focus on the analysis of capitalist production, nature and role of classes, importance of race and gender, role and function of the media, nature of and operation of ideology, fragmentation of community, nature of 'post-industrialism' and the appropriate tactics for revolutionary transformation.

Marxism was developed along pragmatic revolutionary lines by V.I. Lenin prior to the Russian Revolution of February 1917. He continued to develop Marxist–Leninism through the successful October Revolution of that year when the Bolsheviks emerged as the leading party. Marxist–Leninism continually evolved in the following years but after Lenin's death in 1924 gradually became an instrument of state control, especially under Stalin, and increasingly remote from revolutionary practice. Nonetheless, Lenin's contribution to Marxism was taken up and developed within sociology by structuralist Marxists, notably Louis Althusser.

Althusser (1969; Althusser and Balibar, 1970) argued that Marx's writing could be characterised by what he called an epistemological break. Marx's early work was characterised by a humanist approach while his later work was more based on structuralism. A humanist approach places more emphasis on the activities of people and the role of ideology in determining what people do. A structuralist approach places more emphasis on the structures of society and suggests that these play a considerable role in determining what people do.

Althusser strongly argued that a structuralist approach is necessary and that the 'economic relations of production', the way capitalism is organised, is the base of society that determines all other aspects of society, such as education, media, family, religion and so on. These 'superstructure' elements operate to restate and reproduce the productive base: school, for example, educates children as workers on the one hand and as citizens who accept the way capitalism operates on the other.

Two other structuralist influences that fed into Marxist critical social research were developing at the same time: one derived from anthropology, which was encapsulated in the work of Claude Levi-Strauss and the other derived from linguistics, which resulted in the structural linguistics of Ferdinand de Saussure.

Both subscribed to the underlying principle of structuralism, which is that the world is made up of relationships rather than things. This means that the significance of any element cannot be grasped independently of the structure of which it forms a part.

Levi-Strauss, an anthropologist, argued, among other things, that the structure of 'primitive' myths reflects the structure of the society from which they come. By deconstructing the myth, and ignoring all the surplus detail, it was possible to isolate the internal structure of the narrative and show how that reflected the social structure.

Saussure's structuralist linguistics essentially argues that language is an interlocking system. Words do not have any intrinsic meaning. They have no meaning taken in isolation from the language in which they are part. Rather, each word derives its meaning from other words. Furthermore, a word is a carrier of a meaning. Each word consists of two things, a 'signifier', the written word or the sound, and the 'signified', what it relates to. The signifier and the signified combine into a 'sign'. The 'sign' carries the meaning. So the word dog is a sign that consists of a signifier (the three letters D-O-G, which combine into a sound that rhymes with log), and a signified (a hairy quadruped that barks).

Saussure's structural linguistics and Levi-Strauss' study of myths come together in the semiology of Roland Barthes.

SEMIOLOGY

Semiology or semiotics is the theory of signs. More generally, semiology is the study of all patterned communication systems, both linguistic and non-linguistic, for example literature, advertisements, etiquette, ritual and other non-verbal forms of communication such as fashion.

Although rooted in linguistics, semiology has been developed within sociology, particularly in the analysis of the communications media, cultural studies and film studies.

Semiologists argue that signs are arbitrary. However, taking Saussure's notion of the interrelationship of linguistic systems, the underlying assumption of semiology is that as human actions or productions convey meaning there must be an underlying system of conventions and distinctions that makes this meaning possible. The role of semiology is to discover the conventions that make signs what they are.

Sociological semiology seeks to study sign systems and meanings within society. The core of sociological semiology is to uncover the myths or ideology that underlies examples of sign systems. Barthes' approach to semiological analysis of myth works as follows.

1 A sign comprises of two elements: the signifier and the signified, and semiotic analysis is concerned with the relationship between the two, that is, the sign.

2 Barthes argues that a sign contains two meanings, the literal or face-value meaning, known as the denotation (a rose as a flower) and an underlying or interpreted message or symbolic meaning known as the connotation (a rose as symbolising romance). What is being signified is not always self-evident and we need to move from the (first level) denotation to the (second level) connotation.

3 The first stage of analysis is to examine the denoting sign through a deconstruction into signifiers and signifieds. The second stage involves a critique of these denoted signs in order to reveal the connoted symbolism. Finally, these connotations are examined and the myth (or ideology) which underpins these symbolic representations is elaborated.

Barthes' best-known example is a front cover photograph on the magazine *Paris Match*. It was published at the time of the Algerian crisis and showed a black soldier saluting the French flag. Barthes argues that at one level we see the signifier (the photo) and the signified (the soldier saluting) combined into a 'first order' sign of black soldier saluting a flag. At this first level of reading this has no political connotation. At a second level, the first order sign 'black soldier saluting the French flag' becomes the signifier. The signified is 'French imperialism'. This leads to a mythical level (or second level sign) of the 'greatness and impartiality of the French empire, in which all subjects irrespective of colour faithfully serve the French flag'.

Diagrammatically:

A. photo	B. soldier saluting	
C. black soldier saluting flag		D. French imperiality
	E. France is a great empire and all her 'sons' without colour discrimination faithfully serve under her flag.	

A is the first order signifier,
B is signified, C is the sign.
A, B and C operate at the denotative level.
C then becomes the second order signifier, D is signified at the connotative level,
E is the connoted sign.

Study point

Identify three signs and in each case identify the signifier and the signified at the denotative and connotative levels.

This semiological approach enables the 'second level' structure of contemporary mythology to be revealed.

For example, in analysing representation of women, the determination of denotative and connotative meanings allows us to expose the stereotype myths and ideology inherent in statements such as 'take it like a man'. The denotation of which is 'be brave and strong', reflecting the stereotype image of macho men. The connotation is that men, unlike women, are strong, brave, do not let their feelings show – a myth which helps to legitimate the wider ideology of an innate superiority of men over women, which forms the basis of patriarchy.

Activity
In small groups, collect five newspaper or magazine advertisements and analyse them semiotically. What are the underlying myths?

There has been considerable debate about whether it is really possible to make a distinction between denotative meaning and connotative meaning. Stuart Hall (1980) argues that denotation is not as neutral as Barthes suggests, rather the distinction is a useful methodological device to help analyse sign systems to reveal the underlying ideology. Furthermore, the connotation is dependent entirely on context.

Maria Heck (1980) argues, for example, that to use the term 'pig' to connote 'policeman' is effective in limited domains where particular codes or terminology are in use. In a different context, such as feminist dialogue, pig connoted male chauvinist. Thus myth is simply a widespread connotation which has become dominant or hegemonic (in a given context). While the meaning of a sign is contextual, Hall argues that the context is indicative of a domain of 'preferred meanings', which reflect a dominant cultural order. In this way, semiological analysis of mass media is directed towards how the media reflects dominant ideology.

HUMANIST MARXISM

Marx has been criticised by Marxists such as Antonio Gramsci (1971), Georg Lukacs (1971), H. Lefebvre (1984), Raymond Williams (1965) and E.P. Thompson (1963), for placing too much emphasis on (a) the revolutionary mission of the working class (b) class hierarchies and (c) the structure of society. Instead, more emphasis should be placed on the so-called 'superstructural' elements such as education, culture, religion, the media and ideology. In particular, Marx is criticised by Marxists such as Herbert Marcuse (1964) for understating the role of the individual in society.

PROTEST AGAINST GENETICALLY MODIFIED ORGANISMS IN FOOD

The apparent lack of political mission of the working class and an emphasis on culture and ideology rather than structure, led Marxists in the 1960s to focus more on protest movements than working-class organisation. Women's liberation, black movements and middle-class student protests of the 1960s and 1970s have been joined by environmental movements and animal, disability and gay rights as the focus for radical action. In each case, despite some success in getting their concerns onto the political agenda, none of these movements has been the fulcrum for any broad and pervasive political changes. Nonetheless, the grass-roots activities of the late 1980s 'feed the world campaigns' (despite being hijacked by commercial exploitation) reawakened interest in the protest movements of the 1960s and Marxist approaches have tended to operate in a decentralised way. Western European Marxism, in the 1980s and early 1990s was affected by postmodernism, post-structuralism, feminism, anti-colonialism and black critiques of power and moved away from the single model of oppression based upon class alone.

CRITICAL THEORY

One approach that emerged out of the humanist tendency of Marxism was 'critical theory' developed by a group of Marxist academics at the University of

Frankfurt (who became known as the Frankfurt School). Frankfurt School critical theory has subsequently been developed, amongst others, in the work of Jürgen Habermas.

Theodor Adorno was the principal theoretician of the Frankfurt School and he attempted to reintroduce the 'subject' into Marxist analysis. Adorno was also influenced by Nietzsche (a philosopher often seen as one of the early influences on postmodernism, see Chapter 4). Adorno (1976) argued that the task of critical theory was to critique philosophy with a view of developing 'critical social consciousness', that is, to try and understand how social processes and structures actually impose meaning on the individual. The aim of critical theory is to restore an awareness that people are active, yet historically limited, subjects and to try and identify which forms of constraint on human freedom are necessary and which are historically specific.

Habermas argues for a dialectical approach that links the method of Verstehen with causal analytic science but which transcends both through a process of critique that relates theory to history. In this endeavour, Habermas made use of 'hermeneutic analysis'.

Hermeneutic analysis

Hermeneutics is an approach to history that attempts to recreate the meaning of historical events from the available textual data. It does this by using what is known as the hermeneutic circle. This is a complex reflective process that involves:

- reading a historical text;
- trying to identify what it meant in the context of the time it was written;
- using that understanding to reread the text and reinterpret it;
- going round the circle again.

Eventually an understanding of the historical meaning and significance emerges from (or is distilled out of) this process.

Thus, a hermeneutic analysis uses the evolving understanding of history to develop a holistic understanding of the wider context – it places the specific events (or parts) in the context of the whole. This approach had been developed into a critical analysis of history by Hans Jürgen Gadamer. He located the hermeneutic circle of understanding in a wider social context in order to both understand, as far as possible, the historical meaning and to critique the current understanding that historians have of history. In short, Gadamer tried to overcome the way that current views of history actually recreate the 'reality' of the historical past.

Habermas used this notion of *critical hermeneutic* reflection to aid his dialectical analysis of what constituted 'true' knowledge. Paraphrasing Habermas (1987), hermeneutics is a type of inductive process that starts from an initial understanding of specific events or texts (the parts) and proceeds to the attempt to grasp the meaning of the whole. The dialectical element comes in as this initial understanding alternates with an attempt to take the holistic meaning as a basis for defining the parts more clearly. If the individual parts cannot be understood more fully by doing this then the overall grasp of the whole is mistaken and one has to start again. A new holistic reflection is necessary to redefine the meaning of the whole so that it will take account of these parts. This attempt goes on until the entire meaning has been grasped.

Habermas adopted an approach that is on the one hand 'scientific' but also took account of the historical context. This is essentially a process of attempting to place a Verstehen approach to phenomenology in a wider social and historical context.

Knowledge-constitutive interests
Habermas developed Weber's notion of social action and was concerned to identify the kinds of knowledge that could 'truly orient action'. He developed the concept of 'knowledge-constitutive interests', in which he argues that knowledge is not self-evident but constituted according to (that is, based upon) prevailing interests. By interests Habermas meant the rationale for developing knowledge.

Habermas identifies three types of *knowledge-constitutive interests* — the technical, the practical and the emancipatory.

1 Technical knowledge-constitutive interests refer to those aspects of knowledge concerned with manipulation of the environment, of control over natural objects and events. This is close to what we might call applied science.
2 Practical knowledge-constitutive interests are concerned with the 'hermeneutic' task of extending understanding in intersubjective relations, the aim being to achieve consensus, community and mutual understanding.
3 Emancipatory knowledge-constitutive interests are pitched at a more abstract level and involve liberating people from the specific constraints of their particular context (or socio-historical moment, as Habermas called it). This is achieved through 'self-reflection'.

Habermas thus sees critical theory as the basis for rational change via the self-awareness of people, a self-awareness that comes from not only developing knowledge but by analysing the constitutive interests that impinge on the construction of knowledge.

Critical theory and critical social research
It is important not to confuse *critical social research*, which is a broad approach to sociological thinking, with (Frankfurt School) 'critical theory'. Critical theory is a specific theoretical perspective within critical social research, much as structural functionalism is an approach within positivism.

Unfortunately, some commentators give the impression that all critical approaches are dependent on critical theory. For example, Brian Fay's (1987) *Critical Social Science*, despite its title, is primarily an exploration of the critical theory of the Frankfurt School. Martin Hammersley's (1995) positivist critique of critical research also primarily engages with the epistemology of critical theory and fails to address critical social research *methodology*. Similarly, Ben Agger's (1998) *Critical Social Theories: An Introduction* focuses on critical theory and later postmodernist developments.

SOCIAL CRITICISM

Although Marx's work has been developed by later Marxists, there have been other contributors on the edge of the tradition who have contributed to the development of critical social research. In the United States, for example, Marxism has been mostly ignored and it has been left to sociologists such as Robert Lynd (1939) and C. Wright Mills (1956) to develop a critical social research approach with a similar methodological framework but, for political reasons, apparently distanced from Marxist dialectical thinking. Lynd (1939) argued that American social science was characterised by technicians on the one hand, who were obsessed with developing method, and scholars on the other who failed to connect theory with practice. The result was that sociology failed to ask substantial questions, and, instead, constantly looked in on itself.

Having seen no significant change in the 20 years since Lynd wrote *Knowledge for What?*, C. Wright Mills (1973) restated the principles of a critical social research in *The Sociological Imagination*, first published in 1959. Mills couched his reassertion of the need for critical social research in terms of the 'intellectual craftsmanship' of the classic sociological tradition of, among others, Marx, Weber and Durkheim. Sociology, Mills argued, was dominated by abstract theorising on the one hand and detailed but insubstantial method-driven empirical studies on the other. Social phenomena were examined out of context and substantive issues of consequence were no longer the focus of social scientific enquiry. Mills acted as a focal point for a brief revival of an American-style critical social research, variously called 'the new sociology' (Horowitz, 1964) and 'social criticism' (Brown, 1977).

FEMINISM

A significant amount of feminist analysis, although by no means all, comes under the umbrella of critical social research. Historically, feminism has not been homogeneous. On the contrary, it has involved an array of approaches, some of which have involved a critical analysis of the oppression of women and some of which have been based on idealistic notions of the essence of 'female'. Many prefixes, in various combinations, have been added to feminism: socialist,

Marxist, bourgeois, radical, cultural, materialist, idealist, empiricist, positivist, realist, standpoint and postmodernist. Unfortunately, these labels have not been used consistently, nor are they mutually exclusive. What they do suggest is the range of theoretical and epistemological perspectives that underlie different feminist approaches.

Feminism of the 1960s and 1970s grew out of the women's movement and tended to emphasise sisterhood and the personal aspects of social relations. It began, slowly, to address the oppression of women rather than their social disadvantage. Instead of simply campaigning for the equality of opportunity for women in a man's world, the feminists of the 1970s critiqued the prevailing social structure and argued that capitalism and/or patriarchy were at the root of the oppression of women.

Capitalism and patriarchy
There was fierce debate, from the mid-1970s for a decade, about the nature of women's oppression and the appropriate tactics for overcoming it. This debate was multifaceted. Some feminists, often labelled as Socialist feminists, regarded capitalism as the basis of the oppression of women and tended to adopt Marxist or similar approaches to analysing the specific nature of patriarchy within capitalism (Cockburn, 1983; Eisenstein, 1979).

Alternatively, radical feminists regard patriarchy (alone) as the basis of the oppression of women. In short, women are oppressed by men, irrespective of any class oppression.

One version of this (known as idealist radical feminism, biological feminism or, rather inappropriately, as cultural feminism) takes the view that oppression is based on biology. The approach argues that women are biologically different and this leads to psychological differences and women have a view of the world that is ungraspable by men. It is this innate difference that is at the basis of male oppression of females. Such absolutist approaches do not lend themselves to critical social research as they prescribe a causal relationship which is immutable and do not address the social and historical context of oppression.

An alternative radical feminist approach (known as materialist radical feminism) argues that patriarchal oppression is not biological but based on social relations in which males construct society in a way that enables them to hold power over and control women. Materialist radical feminism is amenable to critical social research as it argues that radical changes in social relationships between men and women, and thus radical changes in society, are the only long-term solution to the oppression of women (Delphy, 1985).

Class, gender and race
Class and gender have provided the major axes for feminist critical social research. However, during the 1990s, the issue of race has become more

prominent. The absence of black women from earlier debates cannot be accommodated by simply adding a black perspective to the gender and class analyses that have already been undertaken. Rather, it is necessary to integrate the experiences of black women and to reconstruct an understanding of racially constructed gender roles.

Patricia Hill Collins (1991) argued that black feminist (or Africanist feminist) thought is 'subjugated knowledge' because it cannot be readily expressed in an academy dominated by élitist, white, male thought. She argued that the history of black Africans (slavery, colonialism, apartheid, imperialism) leads to a common Africanist experience of oppression that shapes an Afrocentrist consciousness. This mirrors a similar claim about the development of feminist consciousness from a shared history of male oppression. The parallels between Africanist and feminist experience raise questions about under what circumstances is a black woman's position closer to a white woman's or a black man's? There is, for Hill Collins, no simple answer to this.

Nor, she argued, are black women more oppressed than black males or white females because they supposedly suffer a 'double oppression'. Oppression is not something that you can add up by adding layers. She disagrees with simplistic 'standpoint' approaches that argue that the more subordinated the group the purer the vision of the oppressed group. Hill Collins attempted to define a black feminist epistemology. She argued that an Africanist feminist perspective is characterised by a preference for concrete experience over abstraction and a holistic rather than a dichotomous approach. She also argues that in an Africanist feminist approach people become empowered as a result of dialogue and community leading to harmony.

ANTI-RACISM

Another strand of critical social research comes from approaches that engage racism in one form or another. These approaches are labelled in various ways and the labelling changes rapidly reflecting the politicisation of terms in relation to 'ethnicity' and 'race'. Critical approaches related to 'race' and racism include black Marxism, black sociology (from the US) and anti-colonialism.

One example is Ben Turok's (1987) analysis of the post-colonial situation in Africa. He drew directly on Marxist–Leninism in his exploration of the economic and political situation throughout the continent. He argued that, in order to understand, and ultimately overthrow, the neo-colonialism that characterises most post-independent states, it is necessary to understand the character of the state and the nature of the social superstructure. Although there had been considerable continuity from pre- to post-independence systems, there had, Turok argues, also been a break and it is important to understand the nature of that change. Those who want to change African societies found themselves free from colonial oppression but caught up in a new network of repression and reaction that was often more formidable than the colonial rule. The new internal ruling class, often set in place by the outgoing colonialists to ensure that the interests of the colonial power are safeguarded after independence, was not challenged by mass anti-colonialist nationalist parties. Once power had been handed over to the new bourgeoisie, mass-movement parties were dissolved and with it the opportunity for more power to pass to the mass of the people.

Not all feminist analyses constitute critical social research and the same can be said for analyses of 'race'. Where the analysis is based on a biological reductionist view, that biological differences lead to psychological differences, and thus oppression is based on innate differences, then the causal relationship is fixed and not amenable to critical social enquiry.

Herman Gray's (1989) study of US television's portrayal of black people is an example of an anti-racist critical analysis. He explored fictional television representation of middle-class black people and non-fictional representation of black urban poverty. He argues that the two different portrayals are interwoven (or 'operate intertextually') to produce a dominant ideology. This ideology explains black middle-class success as individual success and the adoption of middle-class values and black urban poverty as the result of structural factors.

Gray uses Stuart Hall's notion of 'preferred level of meaning'. That is, television cannot impose a perspective on the viewer but can suggest an appropriate interpretation of the images and words – that is, the preferred level of meaning. Gray analysed the content of fictional television programmes such as *The Cosby Show* and non-fictional documentaries and showed that the historical realities of black history – slavery, discrimination and racism – are ignored or are translated into a preferred meaning of 'black middle-class visibility and achievement. In this context, successful and highly visible stars like Bill Cosby and Michael Jackson confirm the openness and pluralism of American society' (Gray, 1989, p 431). Conversely, in news accounts, 'the black underclass appears as a menace and a source of social disorganization' with urban crime, drug use, teenage pregnancy, gang violence, riots and homelessness being the main focus of attention.

In nearly all episodes of *The Cosby Show*, the children in the family are given appropriate lessons in 'universal values' such as individual responsibility, parental trust, honesty, the importance of family and the value of education. The personal dimension of social life is emphasised and displaces broader social and structural factors. For Gray, this is all part of ratings wars in television and editorial decisions that are based on the notion that the personal and the 'moral' are more likely to attract viewers. This prioritising of the personal also frames some documentaries on the black urban underclass. For example, a CBS news documentary *The Crisis of Black America: The Vanishing Family* is constructed in such a way that each element of the documentary emphasises individual personalities, aspirations and struggles for improvement rather than social explanations.

> *This displacement of the social by the personal and the complex by the dramatic both draws viewers into the report and takes them away from explanations that criticise the social system. Viewers question individual coping mechanisms rather than the structural and political circumstances that create and sustain racial inequalities' (Gray, 1989, p 435).*

Activity

In small groups, watch (and preferably videotape)

- several television news broadcasts;
- at least one documentary that deals with the lives of black people;
- at least two episodes of a fictional series that features black people.

Examine them to see if the 'preferred reading' identified by Gray is still applicable.

EXAMPLES OF THE CRITICAL APPROACH

Three examples, from different areas, will be used to illustrate the critical social research approach.

CLASSICAL CRITICAL SOCIAL RESEARCH: CAPITALISM

Marx's (1887) last great work, *Das Kapital,* the three-volume analysis of capitalism is a major example of critical social research. A brief review of the analysis in the first volume demonstrates the critical social research way of working.

Marx set out to understand the real nature of capitalism. He could see that capitalism, as the driving force of the industrial revolution, was leading to rapid and massive changes in the 'advanced' countries of the time (England, Germany, France, USA). These changes could be beneficial because of the introduction of many labour-saving machines. However, rather than benefit the workers, capitalism was leading to far worse conditions for workers, with long hours of often dangerous work with very little pay. The capitalists, those people who owned the capital and hired the labour, were the only ones who benefited. So Marx wanted to know why this was, how capitalism really operated. He wanted to get beneath the surface of the workings of capitalism.

He was scornful of religious justifications for inequality or the notion that people were born to different classes and had to put up with their lot.

A COAL MINER IN THE NINETEENTH CENTURY.

Marx was equally scathing of the work of positivist economists of his day who tried to explain the *status quo* in terms of variants of supply and demand. For him, they began in the wrong place. Conventional economics tended to begin with money. He argued that such positivists start with observations and create abstractions to explain them. So, positivists see money as a reality and try and build theories explaining the circulation and accumulation of money. Marx argued that money might appear to be 'real and concrete' but was in fact an abstraction that concealed relations of exchange. His approach was to find the reality beneath the surface of money relations.

He asked, first of all, what was it that was fundamental to capitalism? His answer, after much thought and reflection on the workings of capitalism, was the commodity. In capitalism, everything is a commodity to be bought and sold. Money is not fundamental to capitalism, it is the medium through which commodities are traded. It is the commodity that is fundamental. A capitalist employs workers to use the capital equipment (machines) to make a commodity for the capitalist to sell. So how does the capitalist make money (or accumulate capital, as Marx called it)? A single capitalist could accumulate capital by selling the commodity for more than it was worth. However, *every* capitalist could not sell things for more than they are worth. If they did, then every capitalist would also be buying things for more than they were worth and so the system as a whole could not lead to capital accumulation through sharp selling practices. Capitalists must be accumulating their capital on the basis of something else.

The answer, for Marx, is the commodity. Not only are the products of capitalism (the things that are made) commodities, so too is people's labour. The capitalist buys labour from the labourer, who sells it in order to earn money to live. However, there is a major difference between the trade in commodities and the trade in labour. The capitalist buys the commodity of labour for less than it is worth. The capitalist pays an 'exchange value' for the labour based on the time the labourer spends working. This is different from the 'use value' of the labour, which is the amount of useful products, or commodities, the labourer produces. The capitalist, by paying for the time, has ownership of (or appropriates, as Marx put it) the product of the time spent labouring. In short, the capitalist pays a wage and owns the commodity produced by the labourer. Needless to say, there is a difference between the exchange value of labour and the exchange value of the commodities produced by that labour. The capitalist appropriates the difference (makes a profit out of the labour of others) and labour is exploited.

In effect, the positivist economists of the day argued that the supply of labour was greater than the demand by capitalists so that capitalists were justified in paying low wages. If that situation changed, then inevitably wages would rise. Marx argued that this was a naive, surface argument that simply justified exploitation. It failed to take into account the real historical context and the social structures that had grown up or adapted to support capitalism.

Factories existed in the real world and there was a whole 'ideological superstructure' that supported the capitalists, giving them power to exploit the workers. This ideological superstructure included the church, courts, police and military, newspapers and even academic theorists. They were all, on one hand, creating the illusion that the fate of the workers was to be downtrodden and that they should accept their place in the social order. On the other hand, anyone attempting to do anything about it was subject to the full force of these agencies.

So, capitalism could not just be seen as operating in the factories; economics goes beyond the realms of economic theory. There is a much wider context that includes an array of power relations that have to be taken into account. In short, it is necessary to take into account the 'totality' of social forms.

Marx agreed that there was a class basis to the exploitation of labour but rather than accept that this class differential was inevitable he argued that class structures were not a 'fact of life' but could be torn down. What he advocated was a system in which workers owned their own 'use value', and in that way owned capital in common. Unlike many social scientists today (who think that they should only analyse social situations and avoid any suggestion of action or avoid being implicated in politics) Marx was not afraid that his analysis might lead to social or political action. On the contrary, for him, practical reflective action (or praxis, as he called it) was the inevitable outcome of social analysis. Indeed, praxis was what individuals did all the time. Social analysis might lead to a unified praxis, with people reflecting and acting together to a common end. In the *Communist Manifesto*, Marx and Engels encouraged a whole social class, the workers, to reflect and act to overthrow the bourgeoisie who owned the means of production (that is, the capitalists).

FEMINIST CRITICAL SOCIAL RESEARCH: HOUSEWORK

Christine Delphy's (1978) analysis of housework provides another example of critical social research from a different tradition: feminism. It also shows that critical social research does not solely deal with total systems such as the nature of capitalist economy.

Delphy argues that conventional sociological approaches to examining housework start from the taken-for-granted view that housework is simply a set of specified tasks undertaken in the home, such as cooking, cleaning, ironing, doing the laundry and washing up. She argues that specifying housework in this way reflects the theoretical interpretations that are applied to it.

For example, she refers to the debate, which was topical at the time, that those people who do the housework, mainly women, should be paid a wage. Despite being a feminist, she basically disagrees with this position because, she argues, it misses the point. Similarly, she disagrees with the contrary view that housework is essentially 'free' because, when it is done within the family setting, it is an activity that does not pass through the market. (This does not include the situation where someone pays an outsider to do the housework for them.) If there is no buying and selling of housework within the family then it is an activity without exchange value.

Delphy's view is that these two debates miss the point because they see housework as a set of tasks. As Marx had done in his analysis of money, Delphy argued that housework might appear to be a concrete activity but is actually an abstraction because it, too, concealed relations of production and exchange.

Delphy started by asking what was fundamental about housework. The answer was not that it is a set of 'everyday' activities that take place in the home. On the contrary, what is fundamental to housework is a *relationship of production*. Housework is done by someone for someone else.

Delphy approached this as follows. First she demonstrated that 'payment' and 'remuneration' are not the same. Productive work that one does for oneself does not need payment because the product is itself the remuneration. You get your own benefit for what you do for yourself and do not need paying for it. If the productive work was not done by oneself then, assuming it was required, someone else would have to be paid for doing it. For example, baking and consuming ones own bread is still remunerated through the consumption of the bread. It makes no sense to suggest that the work, as housework, should be paid for as well. Thus not all 'unpaid' work is free. The only 'free' work is when there is no remuneration, that is, when the labourer receives neither payment in exchange for the labour nor payment in the form of self-consumption: in short, when the work is done for someone else. This is the basis of housework, it is unremunerated work done by one family member (the wife in patriarchal families) for other family members. Thus housework is not a set of discrete tasks but 'all the work done unpaid for others within the confines of the household or family' (Delphy, 1985, p 90).

Delphy's analysis illustrates how critical social research takes an empty abstract concept (housework) and shows that it represents a historically specific idea that operates within specific relationships within a social structure – in this case the patriarchal family. By deconstructing the concept of housework and showing that it is not just a 'set of tasks' but a *relationship* of production it reveals the nature of patriarchal exploitation inherent in the abstract concept. It thus provides an alternative way to reconstruct an understanding of housework.

CRITICAL SOCIAL RESEARCH IN CULTURAL STUDIES

There are many critical social research studies of the mass media; many focus on the content of the media (such as Gray (1989) discussed above). Philip Schlesinger's (1978) analysis of the making of BBC news is an example of a critical study of how the content of mass media is produced. Exploring this study we can see how 'traditional' qualitative methods, observation and informal interviews, are combined with a critical theoretical perspective. Schlesinger spent time in studios observing how the news was produced at the BBC but he also linked his observations to a study of the structure, history and ideology of the BBC. From this, he was able to show how the BBC news reproduces 'dominant ideology'.

Schlesinger wanted to find out exactly how the news is compiled in the BBC newsrooms. He wanted to know what determines the stories that are included in the news and the importance given to each. He wanted to see if there was an underlying ideology and whether that led to a specific view of reality being projected through 'the news'.

In addition to direct observation and interviews with BBC news staff, Schlesinger looked at the history of BBC news and the routines that news producers adopted. He examined prevailing myths about news production. Such myths included reporters' belief that they are more-or-less free to collect whatever news stories they think appropriate and the notion that news is somehow produced out of chaos without any noticeable organisational structure. Schlesinger showed that, in fact, news is produced in routine ways and that there are various control systems in operation, such as the process by which stories are allocated to reporters.

THE MAKING OF 'NEWS' CAN BE SUBJECT TO BIAS

Schlesinger's detailed observations shattered the myth of freedom and chaos and he showed that the constraints in place are important in developing and maintaining the BBC's 'world view'. Central to this world view is the notion that news output is 'value-free', and thus unbiased. The result is that there is a 'desired identity' for news workers and all those who work on BBC news conform to it in one way or another. This 'desired' identity of BBC employees was subsequently shown to be 'required' when, in 1985, it was revealed that the government's internal security department (MI5) had an office in the BBC and were actively involved in vetting the selection of journalists and production staff.

However, the reporting of Northern Ireland stretches the credibility of the notion of impartiality. Coverage of Northern Ireland consisted mainly of reports of violence, taken out of context, which failed to analyse the historical roots of the Irish conflict. The treatment of Ireland showed that, while the BBC was not a simple tool of the ruling group (government, army and so on), it was constrained by them and is not entirely independent.

In examining news production, Schlesinger showed that, rather than being strictly impartial, the BBC reproduced the *status quo*. His study linked the process of news production to wider social factors, such as government policy and the need for the BBC to retain the myth of collective neutrality.

Study point

What do these analyses tell you about the role of values in the research process? Use Chapter 2 and the above to help. Can facts be separated from theories?

ELEMENTS OF CSR

All these examples reveal a common approach to thinking sociologically, although they have no common 'methods'. Marx, for example, used documented material, official statistics, newspaper reports; he undertook historical analysis and criticised the work of other academics and commentators. Delphy used her personal experiences, official statistics and economic analyses as well as critiquing other analyses. Schlesinger undertook direct observation and in-depth interviews as well as analysing news output and other documents.

Critical social research does not involve a recipe of processes or a set method of collecting data; official statistics, surveys, document analysis, media analysis, in-depth interviewing, participant and non-participant observation have all been used in CSR. Indeed, CSR ranges across the whole spectrum of sociology and uses a wide variety of different methods of collecting data. Other examples include:

- Paul Willis's (1977) study of schooling, *Learning to Labour*, which used observation and in-depth interviewing;
- Roger Grimshaw and Tony Jefferson's (1987) *Interpreting Policework*, which involved shadowing police on duty;
- Judith Williamson's (1978) *Decoding Advertisements*, which involved analysis of advertisements in magazines and newspapers;
- Will Wright's (1975) *Six Guns and Society*, which involved a systematic analysis of all major western films;
- Sallie Westwood's (1984) participant observation study of female factory workers entitled *All Day Everyday*;
- Theodor Adorno and colleagues' (1982) study of prejudice entitled *The Authoritarian Personality*, which used surveys to explore the roots of fascism.

GETTING BENEATH THE SURFACE

So what does CSR involve? As suggested above, there are many different versions of critical social research. However, there is a common aim which is to *get beneath the surface* of what appears to be going on.

In getting beneath the surface the intention is to uncover alternative ways of thinking about social phenomena. CSR, as we have seen, involves a process of breaking down taken-for-granted conceptualisations of the social world (deconstruction) and building alternative ways of understanding what is going on (reconstruction).

How does CSR do this? By using whatever tool is appropriate and by reflecting on whatever evidence is available.

The key is that CSR involves an intellectual process of *reconceptualisation* aided by an array of evidence that provides alternative ways of thinking. The process is one of taking things apart and rebuilding. Taking things apart is not the same as destroying them. It's like having a Lego house, taking it apart and rebuilding it as a castle. If you want to use the Lego parts to rebuild the castle you have to take the house apart carefully, not simply smash it up with a hammer! Critical social research requires that you carefully take apart existing explanations and rebuild an alternative.

What they have in common, then, is an approach to sociological thinking (Harvey, 1990). This approach has the following conceptual elements:

- abstraction
- essence
- praxis
- ideology
- history
- totality and structure.

This may, initially, seem very complicated. They are strange words and it may not be obvious what they mean. In practice, they are not as complex as they sound and are concepts that bring together theory and method. However, it is important to remember that these elements are not prescriptive tools for collecting evidence, they are the conceptual processes that need to be undertaken by the critical social researcher.

ABSTRACTION

The first element of critical thinking is to turn *abstract* concepts into *concrete* processes. For Marx, an analysis of capitalism only works when 'money' is not seen as an end in itself but as part of a process of capital accumulation and exploitation. Delphy turns the abstract notion of 'housework' defined as a 'set of tasks' into a relation of production, where the wife (usually) does free work for other members of the family. Schlesinger revealed that the abstract notion of 'neutrality', applied to the BBC News, deflected attention from the process by which the News was produced – only certain types of stories get to be in the News and, in the case of the coverage of Ireland, the conflict, which has a long history, is turned into a succession of random and isolated acts of violence.

Jane Hill (1999), in a study of inter-agency cooperation in relation to child abuse, argued that the focus on inter-agency cooperation deflected attention away from the unequal relations in society within which abuses to children take place.

CSR differs, for example, from positivists in the way that abstraction is viewed. Positivists, for example, see abstraction as a process of 'distillation', the abstract concept somehow emerges from repeated observation of the world.

For example, the concept of 'domestic violence' emerges from lots of observations of females being physically abused by their male partners. CSR reverses this taken-for-granted approach to abstraction. CSR argues that 'observations' and 'facts' do not exist independently of their theoretical context (Chalmers, 1994). If 'facts' require a theoretical context in order to have any meaning then concepts cannot be abstracted from them. Unlike positivism, CSR moves from the abstract to the concrete and back again. It takes abstract conceptions and investigates them by putting them in a broader context. For example, aggressive behaviour in the home in which a husband pushes, hits or throws things at his wife is encapsulated by the term 'domestic violence'. CSR goes beyond the surface appearance of domestic violence as a set of aggressive acts and reconceptualises it as, for example, an outcome of a patriarchal control. Viewing domestic violence as a set of acts uncritically assimilates the notion of patriarchal control into the concept – that is, hides it from view. Instead of domestic violence being seen as part of a process of male control of women, seeing it as random acts of violence emphasises individual violence and hides the systematic oppression.

Abstraction, for CSR, is more than specifying the concrete components; it requires identifying and revealing underlying structures, which have been assimilated uncritically into the concept, with the aim of developing a new, reconstructed concept.

ESSENCE

A second element is essence. Essence refers to the fundamental element of an analytic process. Unlike positivists who regard any concern with 'essences' as 'non-scientific', and phenomenologists who seek the essential nature of social processes as an end in themselves, CSR uses essence as a pivotal concept.

Essence is the analytic element that is the key to unlocking the deconstructive process. Marx used the 'commodity form' as a core element in his analysis and critique of capitalist relations of production. Labour is then seen as a commodity, and capitalist accumulation (or profit) results from the labour time being bought for less than it is worth in terms of how much is produced by the labourer in the time. For Schlesinger, the essence of understanding news production was to focus on the 'organisation' of the news. This meant shifting attention away from the myth of the freedom of news reporters to report what they liked.

The essential nature of domestic violence is not the range of aggressive acts as such but the way domestic violence functions within the exploitative relationship of the family unit and as part of the social control of women.

Identifying the essence is not the goal but a step on the way to building an alternative understanding. Marx did not stop when he identified the commodity form as the essential element of capitalism. Instead he used it to show how labourers are exploited. Schlesinger did not stop when he discovered that news reporters were allocated stories, instead he explored the allocation process and examined how allocated stories were interpreted by reporters and editors to fit the acceptable way of presentation that reproduced the idea that the BBC news is impartial.

PRAXIS

A third element is 'praxis', which means 'practical reflective activity'. Praxis is what changes the world. Some critical social research is overt in wanting to change the world. Marx, having analysed capitalism as a process of exploitation, exhorted the workers of the world to take over the means of production and hold capital in common so that they could no longer be exploited. Some critical social research does not make such direct appeals to action. However, critical social research, by its very nature is political. It engages with preconceptions and social structures and shows how an understanding of the underlying processes requires a challenge to prevailing preconceptions and structures.

Reconceptualising domestic violence as really being about the control of women by men shifts the emphasis from the exploration, of say, the cause of a specific incidence of domestic violence to a political issue of power and control. In undertaking such an analysis, CSR fundamentally questions the legitimacy of the familial relationship and the sanctity of 'privacy'. CSR is not afraid of impacting on 'research subjects' by raising consciousness and awareness – in short, by empowering them. For CSR, knowledge is not just about finding out about the world but about changing it.

IDEOLOGY

Ideology is another important element for CSR. Ideology obscures the nature of social relations and power structures. Ideology is an extensively debated and variously defined notion. However, the key aspects of ideology from the perspective of CSR are that ideology reflects a dominant (or hegemonic) world view which serves to legitimate the interests of dominant or powerful groups or classes. Marx argued that the exploitation of labour could not be seen in isolation from the social structure. Apart from the army and police, who could forcibly keep workers under control if necessary, there is a dominant ideology to which the churches, the newspapers and the courts contribute. This ideology reinforces the view that there are some people who, by right, are wealthy and others who have to accept that they are not. Similarly, the ideology that supports the exploitation of women as housewives is summed up in phrases like 'a woman's place is in the home' and 'a woman's work is never done'.

Ideology, essentially, serves to make oppression appear to be natural. Ideology is not merely false consciousness that can be changed by changing people's attitudes. Ideology is constantly reaffirmed on a daily basis and can only be changed through praxis – practical reflective activity on a mass scale. Transcending ideology involves more than just raising consciousness. For example, seeing domestic violence in terms of isolated acts of aggression, reflects a patriarchal ideology that obscures the structural oppression of women. Domestic violence will continue unless it is seen as, at root, about men oppressing women. Unless it is openly vilified and condemned as completely unacceptable by the mass media, religious groups, the courts, the police and so on, domestic violence will continue to flourish as a 'private' sanctioned activity albeit theoretically illegal.

Study point
Why do you think that critical social researchers attach importance to the role of ideology?

HISTORY

History is also an important element in critical sociological thinking. Critical social research does not take place in a vacuum. The subject of critical social research enquiry has a history and this has to be taken into account. History refers to both 'the past' and the *process* of constructing the past. For CSR, history does not already exist as a set of facts. History is an interpretation, which draws selectively on evidence and which is guided by current perceptions. So CSR does not involve simply 'picking up' existing history. Rather it involves digging beneath the taken-for-granted nature of any existing history and to put any apparent 'historical facts' into their social and political contexts, taking account of dominant ideology. A critical study of domestic violence would address the historical evolution of a husband's perceived 'rights' over his wife and explore social and economic changes in the nature of family relations.

TOTALITY AND STRUCTURE

Finally, critical social researchers have also to take into account the interlinked notions of totality and structure. Totality refers to the notion that social phenomena are interrelated and that phenomena should not be analysed in isolation. They are part of a coherent structure that has a history. For CSR, structure refers to the notion of a complex and interdependent set of interrelated components.

Marx argued that you could not see the low wages paid to workers in terms of just the supply and demand of labour. Instead there is a whole interrelated structure of laws, courts, police, churches, social classes, mass media and so on that is organised to ensure that workers are kept under control and accept their position. Schlesinger showed that if one considers wider social factors, such as government policy then the impartiality of the BBC is thrown into question.

Structures are dynamic and should not be confused with fixed 'systems'. A structure embodies a dialectical relationship of part and whole, where the meaning of the totality is dependent on the parts which themselves only have meaning in relation to the whole (the totality). For Marx, capitalism is an evolving structure. Understanding the capitalist process of exploitation requires seeing how the different parts of capitalism relate to each other, how the police, army and courts link to organised religion and mass media and how that relates to the process of capitalist accumulation and oppression of workers.

On a smaller scale, Schlesinger looks at the complex structure that results in the production of news: how government policy, the image of the impartiality of the BBC, the apparent freedom of reporters, the editorial control of news production all come together in the broadcast news.

In adopting a totalistic, structural approach, CSR relates empirical detail to a structural and historical whole.

Domestic violence, for example, is not a set of isolated aggressive acts but the manifestation of a historical relationship in which wives were chattels 'owned' by their husband and where violence continues to be the ultimate expression of power within the family. The tolerance afforded domestic violence, because it occurs in the 'privacy of the home', is part of the wider structure of control of women by men that allows, for example, intimidation of women through the threat of rape and assault if they go out alone at night.

Bunie Sexwale (1994) reported a study of violence committed against female domestic workers in South Africa in the period leading up to the end of apartheid. She draws on the words of the domestic workers. However, she does not just report the harrowing stories as evidence in themselves but sets the experience in the wider context of South Africa's history of colonisation, its apartheid past and the imminent collapse of institutionalised racism. She shows how gender relations involve emotional, sexual and physical violence which goes beyond the personal and are legitimated by structural processes. For example, domestic workers are openly abused and have little or no recourse to legal protection as the police and courts collude with the servant's white employers.

Activity
List the elements of critical social research and write a definition for each of them in your own words. Compare your definition with those of other students in your group.

DECONSTRUCTION AND RECONSTRUCTION

It is important to reinforce that these elements of CSR do not constitute a 'method'. Nor are they simple building blocks that can be constructed into a solution, much less ingredients in a predefined recipe for action. They are interlinked conceptual elements that help us understand the mental process that goes on when doing critical social research. They are drawn together through the process of deconstruction and reconstruction.

Furthermore, these elements of CSR do not favour any specific method of data collection. On the contrary, as we have seen, critical social research is characterised by the use of a wide variety of methods of evidence gathering. In fact, just about every method discussed in Chapter 2 is used in critical social research. The key to approaching 'methods' in CSR is to see them as ways of collecting evidence. It is not the evidence as such that is important (as it is sometimes assumed to be in positivist research, for example, where only 'representative' data is allowed) it is *what is done* with the evidence and how an array of evidence, from a wide variety of sources, enables a process of breaking down apparent explanations or interpretations, and permits the building of an alternative understanding.

Remember, at heart, CSR involves a process of deconstruction (breaking things down) and reconstruction (building alternatives):

- it does it by deconstructing (not demolishing) current perceptions then reconstructing an alternative understanding;
- *abstraction* and *essence* provide clues as to what is really at the heart of the issue;
- *ideology* reminds us of the dominant ways of explaining and accounting for social phenomena;
- *praxis* reaffirms that knowledge is practical and changed by practical action—CSR is overtly political;
- *structure, totality* and *history* provide a reminder of the interrelatedness of social phenomena and the context within which understanding is built.

SUMMARY

- Critical social research (CSR) is a term encompassing an approach to sociological enquiry that attempts to go beneath surface appearance. It attempts to do this by questioning the views of the social world that are usually taken for granted.
- CSR is informed by *critical* epistemology, a view that knowledge develops through critique and is constrained by history and structure.
- Critical social research involves a process of *deconstructing* a dominant understanding and *reconstructing* an alternative understanding that reveals the underlying social and historical interrelationships.
- The dialectical analysis of Karl Marx is the earliest example of critical social research.
- Critical social research is also found in the work of subsequent Marxists, feminists, anti-racists, black sociologists, structuralists, cultural theorists and post-colonialists.
- Some critical social researchers make use of semiology or semiotics which is the theory of signs. Although rooted in linguistics, semiology has been developed by sociology, particularly in the analysis of the communications media, cultural studies and film studies.
- The role of semiology is to discover the conventions that make signs what they are. *Sociological semiology* seeks to study sign systems and meanings within society. The core of sociological semiology is to uncover the myths or ideology that underlie examples of sign systems.
- Critical theory, another form of *critical social research*, was developed by a group of Marxist academics at the University of Frankfurt (who became known as the Frankfurt School). Critical theory has subsequently been developed in the work of Jürgen Habermas.

- Habermas sees critical theory as the basis for rational change via the self-awareness of people, a self-awareness that comes from not only developing knowledge but by analysing the constitutive interests that impinge on the construction of knowledge.
- It is important not to confuse *critical social research*, which is a broad approach to sociological thinking, with (Frankfurt School) 'critical theory'. Critical theory is a specific theoretical perspective within critical social research, much as structural functionalism is an approach within positivism.
- A significant amount of feminist analysis, although by no means all, comes under the umbrella of critical social research.
- Feminism of the 1960s and 1970s grew out of the women's movement and tended to emphasise sisterhood and the personal aspects of social relations. It began, slowly, to address the oppression of women rather than their social disadvantage.
- Class and gender have provided the major axes for feminist critical social research; during the 1990s the issue of race has become more prominent.
- Critical approaches related to 'race' and racism include black Marxism, black sociology and anti-colonialism.
- In the same way that not all feminist analyses constitute critical social research the same can be said for analyses of 'race'.
- Critical social research does not involve a recipe of processes or a set method of collecting data; official statistics, surveys, document analysis, media analysis, in-depth interviewing, participant and non-participant observation have all been used in CSR.
- Critical social research has seven interrelated conceptual elements.

STUDY GUIDE

Group Work

Task 1:

In small groups consider how you would research either football violence, drug usage or dance culture using positivistic, phenomenological and critical approaches. Be prepared to defend your suggestions.

Task 2:

Each member of the group to take one of the concepts listed in Table 5.1 and write a clear definition with some examples. Present these to the group and ensure they are clearly understood by everyone. Answer questions raised in the discussion.

Task 3:

In small groups, try to remember the seven conceptual elements of critical social research. Discuss in what ways are they interrelated? Feed back to the larger group those aspects of critical social research that you find conceptually difficult.

Coursework

Develop an outline of a critical research project that uses a range of methods to explore a substantial issue, such as:

- the impact of charging fees on participation in higher education;
- changes in the right to trial by jury on the civil rights of defendants;
- changes in trade union law on the working conditions and workloads of employees.

Practice Questions

1 To what extent do you think that social research should question the legitimacy of existing social structures?
2 What are the main criticisms that feminists have made of science in general and the practice of social research in particular?

3 Define what is meant by the critical social research approach. Illustrate your answer with examples of sociological studies.

4 Explain what the key differences are between a phenomenological approach and a critical social research approach.

5 What would a researcher who adopted a critical social research approach focus on when studying racism in the police?

6 Assess the view that critical social research provides greater insights to researchers than any single method advocated by either phenomenologists or positivists.

7 Compare and contrast the approaches of critical social researchers, positivists and phenomenologist by using one study from within each tradition.

6

REAL-WORLD SOCIAL RESEARCH

Introduction

THE PROCESS OF undertaking a piece of social research involves the researcher in having to consider several issues. Despite the impression given by many textbooks, social research is not undertaken in a vacuum. The social researcher does not, in practice, have the luxury of deciding on the optimum procedure for developing sociological knowledge through research. On the contrary, external factors impinge on any research project and provide the sociologist with a set of constraints that affect the approach adopted. These constraints include:

- time and money;
- triangulation;
- ethical considerations;
- the purpose and policy implications of the research;
- values and political agendas.

These are the concerns that will be addressed in this chapter. These concerns are relevant to all research approaches but perhaps have been developed more in some than in others.

TIME AND MONEY

The research budget will act as a constraint on the researcher. The amount of time and money available will inform the scope of the research, the sample size and what method or methods can be used. Some methods are more time-consuming and more expensive than others.

For example, a telephone survey of 500 people will be much cheaper and less time-consuming than a survey of 500 people using a structured interview involving the use of researchers travelling to individual houses to conduct interviews.

Similarly, the extent to which it is possible to select a representative sample and obtain a high response rate is often affected by how much money researchers have and how long they have to do the research.

Researchers sometimes like to use more than one data source, method or approach in a research study. This is called triangulation. In part, the decision to use triangulation is based on the amount of time and money available to researchers.

Table 6.1: *Key concepts and questions in this chapter*	
KEY CONCEPTS	KEY QUESTIONS
Triangulation (Denzin, Hochschild, MacDonald)	Why triangulate? What are the different ways of triangulating research?
Ethical issues (MacDonald, Hill, Hammersley & Atkinson, Scully, Maynard & Purvis)	Why are ethical issues important in social research? Who decides on the ethical limits of research?
Informed consent (Polsky, Hill)	Is it important to get the consent of research subjects?
Social policy research	How does social policy research differ from sociological research?
Action research (Stringer, Wheeler, Ben-Tovim)	How does action research differ from other forms of sociological research?
Evaluation research	How effective is policy or research?
Micro politics of research (MacDonald, Bhavnani)	How do micro politics impact on the research process?
Values and political agendas (Devine & Heath, Black)	Why do social researchers need to consider the values and political agendas of funders of research?
Researchers' values and politics (Ben-Tovim)	Can researchers set aside their own politics and values when undertaking social research?
Power relationships (Wheeler, Hammersley, Mauthner & Doucet, Standing)	How do power relations between researcher and subjects affect the research process?
Stereotypes (Eichler)	How can researchers avoid stereotypes?

TRIANGULATION

In its broadest sense, triangulation refers to a combination of ways of exploring a research question. Triangulation can be broken down into four types (Denzin, 1990):

1 researcher;
2 theory;
3 method (or data);
4 methodological.

RESEARCHER TRIANGULATION

Data can be triangulated by comparing the data collected by one researcher with that collected by other researchers using the same methods with different sections of the same sample. In its simplest form, this might be a check on the accuracy of data collected by different members of a team of interviewers. A rather more complex situation occurs when a team of researchers is undertaking participant observation on the same topic in different locations. Different data may be the result of differences in approach by the researchers or genuine differences in the research setting that each is observing.

THEORY TRIANGULATION

Theory triangulation is the analysis and comparison of two or more theoretical positions relating to the research problem. In effect, researchers normally undertake a degree of theoretical triangulation as a matter of course when undertaking a literature review prior to collecting new empirical data. The theoretical triangulation informs the research plan. However, theoretical triangulation may also be used subsequently to help make sense of data that does not seem to corroborate or relate to any individual theory. An example of theoretical triangulation is Hochschild's (1983) study of airline flight attendants, which is based on multiple research strategies and data sources. In the analysis, she moves between interactionists' theories of emotion and Marxian theories of political economy to bring together micro analyses of face-to-face interaction with macro analyses of power, economic and social organisation.

METHOD TRIANGULATION

The different methods discussed in this book are capable of being used on their own. However, the decision to make use of triangulation is sometimes based on the belief of some researchers that no single method will provide a complete picture of the area under study. The use of different methods might occur at different stages of the research or they may be used simultaneously.

For example, a researcher may use focus groups and in-depth interviews to identify the issues relevant to a group of people that will later be surveyed using a structured interview. The qualitative methods are employed at the exploratory stage and the quantitative methods are used to provide statistical indicators and to suggest generalisable relationships between types of respondents and types of answer.

Alternatively, a researcher may, for example, be exploring drug abuse in a small town and might use police records, statistics on convictions, local newspaper reports and non-participant observation all as sources of information to explore the extent and nature of drug abuse. In this simultaneous use of different methods, the researcher has to consider whether the different methods provide different means to getting at 'the data' (also sometimes called 'data triangulation') or whether the different methods are indicative of different methodological approaches that need to be reconciled (methodological triangulation, see below).

Data triangulation is the use of two or more sets of data derived from the same method or different methods. For example, the level of unemployment in a geographical area could be obtained from the Labour Force Survey conducted by the Office of Population Census and Surveys, from unemployment statistics based on the registered unemployed, from statistics estimated by the Low Pay Unit or by a local survey. Each of these figures would be different and, taking into account the limitations of each, it would be possible to triangulate to derive a figure that was as accurate as possible. It also allows the researcher to evaluate the sources by comparing the data collected.

However, the perception of triangulation as 'data triangulation' – that is, that measuring the same research problem from different angles provides you with a better reading or measurement of it – can be a problem. Different data sources are likely to provide information derived from different epistemological or ontological perspectives and thus, implicitly, are data relating to different research questions. 'Data triangulation' also implies a view of the social world in which there is one objective and knowable social reality and all that social researchers have to do is to work out which are the most appropriate triangulation points by which to measure it. Throughout this book we have argued that there are various perspectives that researchers employ and have questioned the notion of there being a single objective social world.

In practice, method triangulation goes beyond 'data triangulation', that is it goes beyond simply using different methods to get at the same thing. More likely, method triangulation involves adopting different methods to look at a research problem from different perspectives, which can be used by the researcher as a means of comparison and contrast.

For example, a case study focusing on drug taking in prison may involve several methods. The researcher could decide to use a questionnaire with staff and prisoners or the researcher could choose to use a variety of methods to collect the data such as, a focus group with prisoners, a questionnaire to all the prison staff and some in-depth interviews with prison officers. Using multi-methods produces different kinds of data on the same topic. In Morag MacDonald's (1999) study, the use of a questionnaire to all staff generated one kind of data and the in-depth interviews and focus groups generated 'rich' (that is, detailed) data by allowing the subjects of the research to raise the points of importance to them.

Furthermore, in this example, constraints of time, resources and access necessitated the use of different methods. For example, using focus groups with prisoners allowed a much wider group to be interviewed than would have been possible if in-depth interviews had been used. In addition, prisons have very regimented schedules and neither the researcher nor the prisoners are able to move around the prison freely. Therefore, it was easier to arrange to have a group of prisoners together in a focus group than to arrange individual interviews (MacDonald, 1997b).

Using a range of methods may also allow the findings from one method to be checked against the findings from another. The use of multi-methods allows findings to be corroborated or questioned by comparing the data produced by the different methods. In the prison research example, the data from the prison officer questionnaires corroborated the data from the prisoner focus groups about the use of drugs in the prison and conflicted with official views about the nature and extent of drug use in prisons.

To sum up, we could argue that researchers may find it helpful to use more than one method in terms of corroborating or questioning their data. Researchers should also be aware that triangulation is not a simple process and findings that come from the use of multi-methods have to be treated cautiously. Furthermore, researchers should not consider that by using triangulation their data is somehow 'proven' or considered to be absolutely correct.

METHODOLOGICAL TRIANGULATION

Methodological triangulation is the most complex issue to resolve. It brings together issues of different techniques, data sources and perspectives of subjects and researchers. Essentially, it requires exploring the extent to which different elements of the data are dependent upon different epistemological presuppositions. Information collected via a questionnaire might be premised on the implicit assumption that it shows broad trends and correlations based on the researcher's perspective of the research problem – an essentially positivist approach. This might be alongside data collected via in-depth interviews that are seeking to get at the meanings of the subjects – a phenomenological approach. How, then are these to be reconciled?

Methodological triangulation is not straightforward in that there is no simple way to resolve epistemological differences. As we stated in Chapter 1, the problem cannot be overcome by assuming that one particular broad method, such as interviewing, is indicative of a particular epistemological framework. For example, the status of the data achieved from an interview is different depending on your perspective. As part of a positivistic approach the interview is seen as a way to gather 'facts' about behaviour or attitudes. (It is likely in this case that the researcher will ensure standardisation in the interviewing process normally using structured interviews with a randomly selected sample.) In phenomenological or critical social research, the interview gives rise to rich data exploring the interviewees' interpretations or understandings, focusing on what the respondents see as the crucial issues. (This type of interview would normally be unstructured or semi-structured and subject to reflexivity rather than verification.) Thus the data produced from the above two interviews may well be very different or even contradictory and it then becomes problematic to decide which set of data takes precedence.

Study point
Does the use of triangulation necessarily improve research outcomes?

ETHICAL CONSIDERATIONS

Ethical issues in social research are about the principles that lay behind what constitutes acceptable research practice. For example, a group of sociologists might be researching the impact that death has on the functioning of the family. However, they may consider it inappropriate to try and interview bereaved family members at the funeral or to turn up at the wake with a video camera recording social interactions. The ethical concerns in this case would be that it would be insensitive, an invasion of privacy and may prolong grief.

When considering ethical questions, it is important to look at the relationship of the researcher to the subjects of the research. Research is about people's real lives and can have a harmful impact on them that lasts longer than the research process. However, researchers should not only take account of the interests and needs of the subjects but also the interests of the wider society.

Ethical issues are complicated and there are few hard and fast rules. The British Sociological Association (BSA, 1996) has a set of ethical guidelines as do many other professional associations. These guidelines are used on a voluntary basis by social researchers. To get approval to undertake a research project researchers sometimes have to submit their proposal to appropriate ethics committees, for example research on prisoners, health and welfare. Ethical issues apply to all three of the approaches to research that have been discussed in Chapters 3–5.

The extent to which ethical issues need to be considered depends on the subject matter of the proposed research. It is important to be sure that no physical or psychological harm will come to those who take part in your research. The importance of confidentiality and the privacy of participants in your research should always be considered. For example, in recent research in Italian prisons it was important that the prisoners, who talked to the researcher about using drugs while in prison, could not be identified as they would face further time in prison if the authorities were aware of their drug-related activity. To guarantee their confidentiality masking techniques were used, such as giving each subject a pseudonym and removing any details that would indicate which prison they were from (MacDonald, 1997a).

Although there are no definitive rules governing ethical behaviour in social research, it is important to be clear about what you regard are your limits of acceptability.

INFORMED CONSENT

When a piece of research is being planned consideration should be given to the issue of informed consent. Informed consent implies that the subjects of the research are aware of the purposes of the research and have agreed to be participants.

In a study in which inter-agency responses to child abuse were explored (Hill, 1999), it was important that the participants were aware that the purpose of the research was not to find fault with the practices of individual professionals. Child abuse is an area where professionals have been particularly susceptible to public criticism. Therefore, the researcher had to be particularly sensitive to the anxieties that could result from her presence at training sessions.

In some circumstances it is neither possible nor appropriate to obtain informed consent. For example, if you are observing how people interact at a football match it is not really feasible to inform the people in the crowd about your research.

Hammersley and Atkinson (1992) argue that the researcher should avoid being deceptive where possible but they acknowledge that this may not always be possible because the aims and purpose of the research may change during the process of the research.

As a researcher, you may be open about doing the research but at the same time it may be necessary to hide your true feelings about the people whom you are researching. Scully (1990), in her study of convicted rapists, had to face a series of ethical issues. She was not open with her research subjects about her true feelings towards them. Rather, she allowed them to see her in a way that would encourage them to talk to her about their crimes of rape:

> *The type of information sought in this research required a supportive, non-judgmental neutral façade – one that I did not always genuinely feel. Frankly, some of the men were personally repulsive… . Indeed some of the interviews required immense effort to remain neutral. But the fact is that no one tells his or her secrets to a visibly hostile and disapproving person.*
> *(Scully, 1990, p 18).*

It is possible that being too open about the research may influence the research subjects and cast doubt on the findings of the research as the subjects may simply give you the answers that they think you want to hear. However, feminist researchers (for example Maynard and Purvis, 1994) have criticised this view and, instead, argue that much research is exploitative and oppressive. Rather than subjects being influenced by open research, the dominant approach is one in which the researcher is in a powerful situation and is able to control and manipulate subjects. Instead, these feminist critics argue that the researcher should be open and honest with the research subjects and, by being *reflexive*, can overcome problems of the effect of the researcher on the research setting.

In this sense, being reflexive involves critically analysing the research process in an attempt to uncover the assumptions about gender, race, disability, sexuality (and other oppressions) which may affect the design, data collection and analysis of research. Oakley, for example, has highlighted the political and ethical issues in the treatment of respondents in survey research in which they are asked identical questions in a set order and where issues raised by the respondents are ignored so as not to disturb the standardised nature of the interview. This criticism is not only confined to survey research but also to conventional participant observation research and unstructured interview studies that prioritise the perspective of the researcher.

Reflexivity is also used in a broader sense (than reflecting on issues of race, class and gender of the researcher) to refer to the process of self-reflection of the researcher about the impact in general that she or he might have on the research setting. For example, to what extent do researchers apply their own interpretations to events, or adopt taken-for-granted perspectives or assume they understand what respondents mean by certain terms or phrases. A good aid to reflexivity is to keep a research diary, which provides a record of continuous self-reflection on the research process.

If the decision has been made not to be open about your presence as a researcher then it is important to consider why you made this decision. Some groups, such as the National Front or a criminal organisation, may be difficult to study if they are aware that they are being observed. However, if you adopt *covert methods* this stops a relationship, based on trust, developing. It may also cause upset to those being studied when they eventually find out (Whyte, 1955). In some cases, covert research may put the researcher in danger (Patrick, 1973). Polsky (1971), who studied deviant activity as a participant observer, is very insistent that even this kind of research should not be covert as it can easily end up with the researcher being compromised and it is almost impossible to maintain a role as a covert participant observer over a long period of time.

Although the issue of covert research is particularly acute for participant observers, it occurs in a less obvious form in nearly all research. For example, a standard survey of employee satisfaction may appear to be designed to find out what aspects of work employees are happy about and which cause concern. However, if the researcher is, for example, secretly linking responses of workers to the managerial style of their managers, then there is a covert element that is unknown to the respondents.

When you are planning and undertaking your research you should, periodically, ask yourself the following questions in order to ensure that your study is ethical.

1 Are the methods I have chosen ethically justifiable?
2 Have I provided enough information about the research for my research subjects to give informed consent?
3 Can I ensure the confidentiality and privacy of my research subjects?
4 Who is sponsoring the research and what effects will this have on the likely outcomes and findings of the research? What is the likely audience of the research?
5 Have I set up support for the research subjects if they become distressed talking about sensitive issues in their lives? In addition, how will I, as the researcher, receive support discussing potentially distressing subjects?
6 Have I considered who will benefit from the research? Are the outcomes of the research worth the possible disruption to people's lives?
7 Have I considered the likely responses to my research findings when they are published and become public property and no longer within my control? What can I do if the research is used for purposes that I do not approve of or anticipate?

Study point
In small groups consider what you think are the ethical issues raised in the following example. You have been asked by a large Health Authority to research why there is a high rate of teenage pregnancies in the inner city area and to make recommendations for the Health Authority's future Family Planning Budget.

PURPOSE AND POLICY IMPLICATIONS OF THE RESEARCH

SOCIAL POLICY RESEARCH AND SOCIOLOGICAL RESEARCH

There is a tendency within sociology to distinguish between sociological research and social policy research. However, the literature tends to infer a difference rather than be clear exactly what the difference is. In one sense, the distinction is artificial and tends to represent an idealised version of the optimum sociological research process. This idealised notion of sociological research is contrasted with policy research, which is somehow tainted by dealing with immediate policy concerns. In practice, the distinction between social policy research and sociological research tends to be pragmatic and, often, retrospective. The pragmatic distinction tends to be based on questions such as the following:

- is the research linked to a current social policy issue?
- is it a study of a 'social problem'?
- is it funded by a government department or a policy-based agency?
- is there a relatively short time frame in which to produce a report?
- is the expected outcome a report (which may remain private) to the sponsors?
- will the report avoid addressing complex theoretical issues?
- will the report contain recommendations for action?

If the research is characterised by most of these elements then it is likely to be labelled as social policy research. However, to divide sociological work into sociological research and social policy research is misleading, for several reasons.

First, the policy and non-policy research is often carried out in the same way; it is only the style of reporting and, sometimes, the time frame that is different.

Second, although the research specification and funding may direct the research towards a policy goal, sociologists are flexible and may use the research outcomes for a variety of purposes, including theoretical development as well as policy recommendations.

Third, social policy is not atheoretical, even if the reporting of the research does not labour or make explicit theoretical debates.

Thus, the distinction between social policy research and sociological research turns out to be rather vague. Rather than see social research in terms of this simple dichotomy, it is perhaps more appropriate to explore the different types of purpose of sociological enquiry.

PURPOSE OF THE RESEARCH

Research has a range of purposes including to:

- develop theory;
- inform policy;

- provide further insight or elaboration;
- raise awareness;
- evaluate processes.

If the central purpose is to *develop theory* then the approach may be 'purist' in the sense that it aims to add to theoretical debates and to become part of the 'sociological literature'. If this is the case then the main output will probably be an academic article in a theoretically oriented journal or a research monograph, possibly followed by a book.

If the research is to *inform policy* then the approach may be more eclectic with a view to persuading policy-makers to amend policies or adopt new policies. The output is likely to be a report, written with the potential audience in mind, including clear indications of appropriate action at the policy level.

The research may, of course, be done with neither of these as the primary motivation. It might be research to address a particular social issue, with the aim of providing *further insight or elaboration* of a sub-area of sociology. For example, it may be research to update existing literature in the light of changes, for example in communication technology. There are, for example, many studies of the way children respond to television but most of this was based on research that took place before satellite, cable and digital television were available.

The research might be to raise awareness and may take the form of *action research* or it may *evaluate* policy or the effectiveness of a research project.

Action research
Action research has been defined (Stringer, 1996, p xvi) as involving processes that:

- are rigorously empirical and reflective (or interpretive);
- engage people, who have traditionally been called 'subjects', as active participants in the research process;
- result in some practical outcome related to the lives or work of the participants.

Community-based action research has been used in a wide range of areas, for example in schools, government departments, factory workers and people suffering from particular illness or disability. In action research, the researcher is not just seen as a researcher but also as a resource person:

he or she becomes a facilitator or consultant who acts as a catalyst to assist stakeholders in defining their problems clearly and to support them as they work toward effective solutions to the issues which concern them (Stringer, 1996, p 22).

An example of an action research project is Wheeler's (1994) exploration of service provision for black mental health service users. Local authorities, health authorities and family health services have a statutory responsibility to provide 'care in the community' for individuals who have been discharged from psychiatric hospitals. Wheeler set out to examine the nature and extent of this care for black and ethnic minority groups. The research is action research because she actively lobbied on behalf of, and informed her respondents about, policy issues throughout the course of the research.

> *What was necessary and, fortunately, an integral aspect of this particular piece of research, was to be able to speak on behalf of service users and carers in a critical but constructive way at statutory sector forums, while the research was in progress. In this way one could lobby for changes before the completion of the research project, and keep voluntary sector organizations and black and ethnic minority professionals informed of findings, which they in turn could use to exert pressure for changes in service provision (Wheeler, 1994, p 56).*

Similarly, Ben-Tovim *et al.*, (1986) undertook action research in Liverpool and Wolverhampton looking at the political processes that gave rise to racial inequalities. They considered policy implications of their work as an integral part of the research, not an appended afterthought. Their action research involves an ongoing lived experience that provides the basis for a constant reformulation, elaboration and development of research problems.

Evaluation research
Research might also be designed to *evaluate* the procedures or practices that organisations adopt, for example the implementation of an environmental policy by a local authority, or the effectiveness and impact of a 'no smoking' policy in a large organisation.

It might even be evaluation of a policy-related research project, for example an evaluation of whether a research initiative designed to provide better links between higher education institutions and small firms might be evaluated to see if the initiative actually delivered closer ties. In this case, the research focuses specifically on evaluating a policy or a project and the outcomes will tend to be a written or oral report (or both) that sets out the original intentions of the project or policy and details the evidence to suggest that it has, or has not, worked.

In addition, a typical evaluation report will usually outline any unintended consequences and suggest what general lessons can be learned that would apply in other areas or might lead to changes in subsequent policy or projects.

In conclusion, there are several reasons for doing research and they may or may not be closely linked to policy or theory. However, policy or theory are not alternatives, rather most research will contain elements of both to different degrees. Indeed, empirical research is usually so expensive and time-consuming that the information is often used in a variety of ways and, in practice, much research will be used for more than one purpose.

VALUES AND POLITICAL AGENDAS

We have argued that sociological research, be it policy-oriented or not, does not take place in a social and political vacuum but that values and politics are factors in the research process. This view is endorsed by Fiona Devine and Sue Heath who argue that 'social research in an inherently political act' (Devine and Heath, 1999, p 114). The politics of research operates at two levels: the 'micro politics' of the research process and the wider (macro) political and social context in which the research is situated. The latter is reflected, often, in the values and political agendas of the people funding the research and the politics and values of the researchers. In practice, the micro politics of the research process and the macro politics of the research context are interrelated.

MICRO POLITICS OF RESEARCH

The micro politics of research refers to the political sensitivity that researchers need in their everyday engagement with others whilst doing the research. In this sense, 'politics' does not mean party politics or national politics but the political agendas of individuals or organisations.

For example, you may be researching likely future changes in organisational structure and, as part of that, interviewing people in a sample of institutions. If any of the people you are interviewing feel that their job is insecure they may provide responses to questions designed to safeguard their jobs.

When undertaking research into prisons, Morag MacDonald (1999) had to be aware of the complexities of overlapping portfolios and lines of communication within the Italian system so as not to accidentally offend anyone who might be able to vouch for her research or provide access to prisons.

The micro politics of research also needs to be addressed within the researcher-subject relationship. Kum-Kum Bhavnani (1994) reflects on her experiences of interviewing young black people and, as a black female researcher, of interviewing young white men. Her study contained 72 young people, of which one-third were of Afro-Caribbean origin, one-third were of south-Asian origin and the remaining third were white. She points out that the ascribed characteristics of race, gender, class and age of herself as the researcher and her subjects had an impact on the research. She ignored the idea of matching the characteristics of interviewer and interviewed because she wanted to see what would happen during the interviews. She argued that matching

> *can take the gaze of the analyst and reader away from the micro politics of the research encounter. This is because matching...cannot explicitly take account of the power relations between the researcher and the research, and yet both processes imply that unevenness between the two sides in a research study has been dealt with (Bhavnani, 1994, p 54).*

For Bhavnani, it is important that the micro politics of the research are analysed, not just noted.

VALUES AND POLITICAL AGENDAS OF FUNDERS

For research to take place at all there needs to be certain social, economic and political conditions present. The decision whether to fund certain research studies depends on a range of value judgements as do the decisions to allow access to information, documents and key informants.

Before the research begins, an important stage is the defining of problems considered to be worthy of being researched. It is important, in theory, that researchers should be involved in the identification and defining of research problems utilising their professional skills and different perspectives rather than rely on the potential vested interests of community groups or other professional groups. An important and interesting part of the process of identifying the research problem for the researcher, is to deconstruct how social problems come to be defined as problems by the organisation or group. However, how a problem becomes defined is not always apparent or straightforward and the problem may be defined independently of, or irrespective of, the input of any social researchers. The researcher may, in practice, respond to a 'tender' for a research project, in which the funder has already predefined the nature of the problem.

Problems, for example, may be identified in an institution or organisation by those who work in them and then money is made available to employ researchers to look for solutions. This is often the case in *evaluation* research but is also increasingly the case in all types of social research as there is a growing tendency for funders, such as research councils and charitable foundations, to specify the research areas that they are willing to fund.

Furthermore, obtaining funds to carry out research on a particular subject area can be problematic if the academic establishment does not consider a particular topic to be a worthy subject for research. For example, the academy defines what is a suitable topic for funded PhD research. In the 1960s, for example, Anne Oakley came up against this problem when she experienced some difficulty in finding a supervisor for her proposed research on housework. At the time, housework and the work that women do in the home was not considered to be of sociological interest.

Another example of institutionalised hostility to research is documented by Naomi Black (1987) who moved from international relations into the study of women and politics. She faced considerable hostility from male colleagues who accused her of doing propaganda instead of political science. Male colleagues, who had never been asked to justify their own work, accused her of doing research when she already knew the answers.

Similarly, Marshall (1994) argues that the process of carrying out research in universities is particularly difficult for black women because 'we occupy an outsider within status'. Patricia Hill Collins, however, asserts that the unique 'insider–outsider' position of marginalised black feminist researchers allows her to 'recognise the ramifications that those of the dominant culture are unable to comprehend'.

The idea of doing feminist research assumes that those involved in the research have the same power in, and hence control over, the research hierarchy. However, many women working within research are at the bottom of the research hierarchies where they have little control over the research process and the analysis and interpretation of data.

Access to information and powerful groups
Information that is required for research is often expensive and not always easily available. The control of such information is a source of power. Even when access is allowed to the information, those who hold the power can also control the publication of any research findings. An example of this is government agencies, such as the Home Office, who can control publication of findings by asking researchers to sign the Official Secrets Act.

It is much easier to research groups who have little power, like women, 'deviant' groups (gangs, drug addicts and so on), working-class people and students. It becomes much harder to gain access to groups who hold powerful positions like the police, the army, politicians, and managers of multinational corporations because they can make access very difficult for researchers. It should also be remembered that funding for research often comes from these powerful groups. Hence, researchers need to be aware of the implications about collecting data from individuals and providing powerful institutions with this data to be used in ways not considered ethical by the researchers.

VALUES AND POLITICS OF RESEARCHERS

Research is affected by researchers' values, which are formed from the researcher's gender, ethnicity, culture, sexuality and a range of other factors. Researchers' values direct the way a problem is defined and the ways in which it is subsequently researched. Researchers' values will influence the epistemology adopted in the study.

Although many social researchers acknowledge that research is a political process, at the macro as well as the micro level there are still some who continue to argue that research should strive to be objective, value-neutral and non-partisan. Throughout this book we have argued against this view (see Chapter 2). Ben-Tovim *et al.*, (1986) went further and argued that not only is social research political but that the social researcher should be explicit about their political standpoint. They argue that:

The tendency to divorce research from its would-be political context and to abstain from researched-based interventions in politics has only served to sanction the political status quo *and in some instances no doubt to actually exacerbate inequalities themselves.*
(Ben-Tovim *et al.*, 1986, p 5).

The issues of power and politics in the research process also relate to the power imbalance between the researcher and those being researched.

Researcher–researched relationship

Whatever the intentions of the researcher, it is very difficult to reach a situation in which the power relationships between the researcher and the researched are equal. Wheeler (1994, p 56) commented on the imbalance between interviewer and interviewee in her action research. She felt that the interviews she undertook were intrusions into the lives of the respondents because she was 'taking away something from them' but was not able 'to give anything immediate or tangible in return, or to give any guarantees about service improvements'.

Hammersley (1995), on the other hand, does not see this imbalance in power between the researcher and the researched as problematic. He does not agree with the assumption that research has, or should have, a central role in the lives of those being studied. This further illustrates the point that researchers have to consider their own research styles and what they consider to be ethical ways of conducting the research process.

Despite the efforts some researchers make to try to give voice to respondents it is almost impossible to avoid the differences in power between the researcher and the researched. In the end, the researcher has the ultimate power to decide how to use the information gathered. For example, at the analysis stage, the researcher makes decisions that affect how the research conclusions turn out.

This is of more concern in situations when it is people with little access to power who are the subject of the research. As noted earlier, more powerful groups and agencies have the power to control the findings of research. During this analysis stage, respondents are disempowered because it is the researcher who makes choices and decisions about the respondents' lives. The researcher chooses:

which particular issues to focus on in the analysis: how to interpret their words: and which extracts to select for quotation. We dissect, cut up, distil and reduce their accounts, thereby losing much of the complexity, subtleties and depth of their narratives. We categorize their words into overarching themes, and as we do so, the discrete, separate and different individuals we interviewed are gradually lost.
(Mauthner and Doucet, 1998, p 138).

Inclusivity
The issues of power and politics in research do not come to an end once the data has been collected but continue into the analysis and writing up of the research. The way we use language will represent power relations and may also silence groups who are less powerful. As Kay Standing (1998) argues:

There is a need to challenge the use of academic language to find new ways of writing and new methodologies that do not exclude and alienate. Research does not take place in isolation; the use of language and the issues of power involved are situated within specific cultural, historical and ideological circumstances which influence our writing and use of language.
(Standing, 1988, p 198).

Furthermore, many researchers are now making more effort to ensure that their research does not exclude groups within society by either ignoring them totally or using sexist or racist language.

It is important that social researchers do not use racist or sexist stereotypes. Researchers need to be careful not to use categories (such as 'women', 'blacks', 'disabled') without specifying who is included within each category. If this is not done the diversity of people's experiences become lost. For example, within the category 'women', black women's experience of the labour market would be very different to that of white, middle-class women.

Eichler (1988) offers some non-sexist research guidelines:

- Avoid sexism in titles. This includes both avoiding sexist language such as 'The Policeman on the Beat' and misrepresentation such as *The Affluent Worker* (Goldthorpe *et al.*, 1968), which should have been called 'The Male Affluent Worker'.
- Eliminate sexism in language: it should be clear when men *or* women are being referred to and when *both* are being referred to.
- Eliminate sexist concepts: for example do not define class by the head of household.
- Reduce sexism in design of research by including both men and women where it is relevant to do so.
- Eliminate sexism in methods.

- Eliminate sexism in interpretation.
- Eliminate sexism in policy evaluation so that policies serve the needs of both men and women.

The use of language is not neutral and value-free and dominant ideologies can be reproduced or challenged by careful use of language, making categorisations clear and avoiding sexist and racist language.

CONCLUSION

As we have seen from the discussion, politics and power affect which subject areas come to be researched, how they are researched and by whom. Access to funding is partly dependent on how important the topic is considered to be by the various funding agencies and partly on how government policy is formulated in terms of the funding made available to support academic research more generally.

The moral and political values of researchers also affect the way in which a research problem is conceptualised and researched. In addition the social identity of the researcher – their social class, ethnicity and gender – impacts on the research process.

The researcher's social identity, access to funding bodies, gatekeepers and information will affect the kind of knowledge produced from the research. This demonstrates the importance of researcher reflexivity. Preconceptions and the effect of the researcher on the research situation constantly need to be considered.

SUMMARY

- Social research is undertaken in real-world settings and thus researchers are faced with a range of constraints. These include: the time and money available, decisions about the need for triangulation, ethical considerations, the purpose and policy implications of the research and the values and political agendas of the researchers, the researched and the commissioners of the research.
- The research budget and the available time will limit the choice of method and approach that can be used.
- Triangulation may be adopted in a research project to provide alternative ways of exploring an issue. Triangulation takes four forms: researcher, theory, method (or data) and methodological.
- Ethical issues in social research are about the principles to be applied when undertaking research. When considering ethical questions, it is important to look at the relationship of the researcher to the subjects of the research so as to

avoid impacting negatively on people's lives. The importance of confidentiality and the privacy of participants should always be considered in a research project.

- Researchers should ensure, where feasible, that informed consent is obtained, and should also avoid being deceptive where possible.
- Research is sometimes divided into social policy research and sociological research, depending on its apparent purpose.
- Research purposes include: the development of theory, informing policy, provision of further insight or elaboration, raising awareness (including action research) and evaluation of processes.
- Values and politics are factors in the research process. The politics of research operates at two levels, the 'micro politics' of the research process and the wider, 'macro' political and social context in which the research is situated.
- The micro politics of research refers to the political sensitivity that researchers need whilst doing the research. It is concerned with the political agendas of individuals or organisations.
- Macro politics refers to the values and political agendas of funders and the values and politics of the researcher.
- The political values of funders or enablers of research relates to the decisions about why the research is being funded and what the commissioners are looking for.
- The values that are formed from the researcher's gender, ethnicity, culture, sexuality, world-view and a range of other factors direct the way a problem is defined and the ways in which it is subsequently researched. Researchers' values will influence the epistemology adopted in the study. It also impacts on the power relationship between researcher and researched.

STUDY GUIDE

Group Work

Task 1:

Each group should, first, list the advantages and disadvantages of different types of triangulation and then design a project that uses triangulation to research one of the following topics:

- drug misuse in schools;
- football violence at international matches;
- community policing in a small town;
- the impact of tourism on the environment in a location of your choice.

Task 2:

Each member of the group to take one of the concepts listed in Table 6.1. Provide a detailed definition with examples. Make a brief presentation to the group and answer questions.

Coursework

Use a range of methodologies to examine changing attitudes towards feminism. Assess the strengths and weaknesses of each and how far they combine to provide more insight than could be obtained with any one method.

Develop a project based on the topic areas outlined in Group Work, Task 1, above.

Revision Hints (see also general hints in Chapter 2)

Discuss the idea of triangulation with someone who knows nothing about the issue involved. Make clear how a researcher would undertake a project that involved at least one form of triangulation.

Practice Questions

1 'All social research involves making ethical decisions.' Outline and discuss the ways in which sociologists need to consider ethical issues in their research. Use examples to illustrate your answer.

2 Is it meaningful to draw a distinction between social policy research and sociological research? Give reasons for your answer.

3 What factors influence the sociologists' choice of quantitative or qualitative methods of research?

4 How might researchers' values and politics affect the research they are undertaking?

FURTHER READING

Adorno, T.W., *et al.*, 1982, *the Authoritarian Personality*. In collaboration with Aron, B., Levinson, M.H. and Morrow, W., New York, Norton.

Adorno, T.W., *et al.*, 1976, *The Positivist Dispute in German Sociology*. Translated by Adey, G. and Frisby, D., London, Heinemann.

Afshar, H. and Maynard, M., (Eds.) 1994, *The Dynamics of 'Race' and Gender: Some feminist interventions*. London. Taylor & Francis.

Agger, B., 1998, *Critical Social Theories: An introduction*. Colorado, Westview Press.

Althusser, L. & Balibar, E., 1970, *Reading Capital*. London, New Left Books.

Althusser, L., 1969, *For Marx*. Harmondsworth, Allen Lane.

Atkinson, 1977, 'Societal reactions to suicide: the role of the coroners' definitions' in Cohen, S. (Ed.) *Images of Deviance*. Harmondsworth, Penguin.

Bauman, Z., 1990, *Thinking Sociologically*. Oxford, Blackwell.

Ben-Tovim, G. Gabriel, J., Law, I. and Stredder, K., 1986, *The Local Politics of Race*. London, Macmillan.

Bennet, T., 1988, 'An assessment of the design, implementation and effectiveness of neighbourhood watch in London', *Howard Journal of Criminal Justice*, 27(4), pp. 241–55.

Bhavnani, Kum-Kum, 1994, 'Tracing the contours: feminist research and feminist objectivity', in Afshar, H. and Maynard, M., (Eds.) 1994, *The Dynamics of 'Race' and Gender: Some feminist Interventions*. London. Taylor & Francis, pp. 26–40.

Black, N., 1987, '"The child is father to the man": the impact of feminist on Canadian political science', in Tomm, W. (Ed.) *The Effects of Feminist Approaches on Research Methodologies*. Waterloo, Wilfred Laurier University press, pp 225–43.

Blackwell, A. and Harvey, L., 1999, *Destinations & Reflections: Careers of British art, craft and design graduates*. Birmingham, Centre for Research into Quality.

Blumer, H., 1969, *Symbolic Interactionism: Perspective and method*. Englewood Cliffs, Prentice-Hall.

Bowling, B., 1998, *Violent Racism, Victimization, Policing and Social Context*. Oxford, Clarendon Press.

British Sociological Association (BSA), 1996, *Guidance Notes: Statement of ethical practice*, document reference: misc/ethgu2.doc. Produced by the BSA, address: tunit 35/G Mountjoy Research Centre, Stockton Road, Durham DH1 3UR. E-mail britsoc@dial.pipex.com

Brown, R.H., 1977, *A Poetic for Sociology*. Cambridge, Cambridge University Press.

Bulmer, M., 1984, *The Chicago School for Sociology: Institutionalization, diversity and The rise of sociological research*. Chicago, University of Chicago Press.

Cain, M., 1993, '*Foucault, feminism and feeling: what Foucault can and cannot contribute to feminist epistemology*' in Ramazanoglu, C., *Up Asgainst Foucault: Explorations of some tensions between Foucault and feminism*. London, Routledge.

Chalmers, A.F., 1990, *Science and its Fabrication*. Buckingham, Open University Press.

Chalmers, A.F., 1994, *What is this thing called Science?* Milton Keynes, Open University Press.

Charlesworth, S.J., 2000, *A Phenomenology of Working-Class Experience*. Cambridge, Cambridge University Press.

Cockburn, C., 1983, *Brothers: Male dominance and technological change*. London, Pluto.

Cotterill, P., 1994, *Friendly Relations? Mothers and their daughters-in-law*. London, Taylor & Francis.

Craib, I., 1992, *Modern Social Theory*. Hemel Hempstead, Harvester Wheatsheaf.

Delanty, G., 1997, *Social Science: Beyond constructivism and realism*. Buckingham, Open University Press.

Delphy, C., 1978, 'Housework or domestic work?' in Michel, A., (Ed.), 1978, *Les Femmes dans la Société Marchande*. Paris, PUF. (Republished in Delphy, 1985, pp. 78–92).

Delphy, C., 1985, *Close to Home*. London, Hutchinson.

Denzin, N. (Ed.), 1990, *Studies in Symbolic Interaction*. Number 11.

Devine, F. and Heath, S., 1999, *Sociological Research Methods in Context*. Basingstoke, Macmillan.

Douglas, J.D., 1967, *The Social Meanings of Suicide*, Princeton, Princeton University Press.

Duffield, M., 1988, *Black Radicalism and the Politics of De-industrialisation*. Aldershot, Avebury.

Eichler, M., 1988, *The Double Standard. A feminist critique of feminist social science*. London, Croom Hill.

Eisenstein, Z. (Ed.), 1979, *Capitalist Patriarchy and the Case for Socialist Feminism*. New York, Monthly Review Press.

Eliasoph, N., 1998, *Avoiding Politics: How Americans produce apathy in everyday life*. Cambridge, Cambridge University Press.

Ely, M. *et al.*, 1997 *On Writing Qualitative Research: Living by words*. London, Falmer.

Fay, B., 1987, *Critical Social Science: Liberation and its limits*. Cambridge, Polity.

Foucault, M., 1977, *Discipline and Punish*, London, Allen Lane.

Fuller, S., 1997, *Science*. Buckingham, Open University Press.

Garfinkel, [1967], 1984, *Studies in Ethnomethodology*. Cambridge, Polity.

Giddens, A., 1976, *New Rules of Sociological Method: A positive critique of interpretative sociologies*. London, Hutchinson.

Giddens, A., 1984, *The Constitution of Society*. Cambridge, Polity.

Goldthorpe, J.H., Lockwood, D., Bechofer, F. and Platt, J., 1968, *The Affluent Worker: Industrial Attitudes and Behaviour*. Cambridge, Cambridge University Press.

Gramsci, A., 1971, *Selections from Prison Notebooks*. London, Lawrence & Wishart.

Gray, H., 1989, 'Television, Black Americans, and the American dream' in, Dines, G. and Humez, J.M. (Eds.), 1995, *Gender, Race and Class in Media*. London, Sage, pp. 430–7.

Grimshaw, R. and Jefferson, T., 1987, *Interpreting Policework: Policy and practice in forms of beat policing*. London, Allen and Unwin. [ch. 5]

Habermas, J., 1987, *Knowledge and Human Interests*. Translated by Shapiro, J.J. Cambridge, Polity.

Hall, S., 1998, 'Encoding/Decoding' in Hall, S., Lowe, A. and Willis, P. (Eds.), *Culture, Media, Language*, London, Hutchinson, pp. 128–39.

Hammersley, M. and Atkinson, P., 1992, *Ethnography: Principles in practice*. London, Tavistock.

Hammersley, M., 1995, *The Politics of Social Research*. London, Sage.

Hardin, S., 1991, *Whose Science? Whose Knowledge?* Milton Keynes, Open University Press.

Harvey, L. and MacDonald, M., 1993, *Doing Sociology: A practical introduction*. London, Macmillan.

Harvey, L., 1987, *Myths of the Chicago School of Sociology*. Aldershot, Avebury.

Harvey, L., 1990, *Critical Social Research*. London, Unwin Hyman/Routledge.

Heck, M., 1980, 'The ideological dimension of media messages' in Hall, S., Hobson, D., Lowe, A. and Willis, P. (Eds.), 1980, *Culture, Media, Language*. London, Hutchinson, pp. 122–7.

Hester, S. and Eglin, P., 1992, *A Sociology of Crime*. London, Routledge.

Hill, Collins, P., 1991, 'Toward an Afrocentric feminist epistemology', in Fornow, M. and Cooke, J. (Eds.), 1991, *Black Feminist Thought: Knowledge, consciousness, and the politics of empowerment*. New York, Routledge, Chapman and Hall.

Hill, J., 1999, The discourse of inter-agency co-operation: towards a critical understanding of the theory and practice of child protection work. University of Keele, Ph.D Thesis.

Hobbs, D., 1988, *Doing the Business: Entrepreneurship, the working class and detectives in the East End of London*. Oxford. Oxford University Press.

Hochschild, A., 1983. *The Managed Heart*. Berkeley, University of California Press.

Hood, R., 1992, *Race and Sentencing*. Oxford, Clarendon Press.

Horowitz, I.L. (Ed.), 1964, *The New Sociology. Essays in social science and social theory in honor of C. Wright Mills*. London, Oxford University Press.

Ingrisch, D., 1995, 'Conformity and resistance as women age' in Arber, S. and Ginn, J. *Connecting Gender and Ageing*. Buckingham: Open University Press.

Jones, P., 1993, *Studying Society*. London, Collins Edel.

Kristeva, J., 1984, *Revolution in Poetic Language*, New York.

Kuhn, T., 1970, *The Structure of Scientific Revolutions*. Second edition. Chicago, Chicago, University Press.

Lacan, J., 1968, *The Language of the Self: The function of language in psychoanalysis*. Translated by Anthony Wilden. Baltimore, John Hopkins University Press.

Lazarsfeld, P. and Rosenberg, M., (Eds.) 1955; *The Language of Social Research: A reader in the methodology of social research*. New York, The Free Press.

Lazarsfeld, P., Pasanella, A. and Rosenberg, M., (Eds.), 1972, *Continuities in the Language of Social Research*. New York, The Free Press.

Lefebvre, H., 1984, *Everyday Life in the Modern World* (trans. S. Rabinovitch). New Brunswick, NJ, Transaction.

Lukacs, G., [1923] 1971, *History and Class Consciousness: Studies in Marxist dialectics*. London, Merlin.

Lynd, R., 1939, *Knowledge For What?* Princeton, NJ, Princeton University Press.

Lyotard, J-F, 1984, *The Postmodern Condition: A report on knowledge*. Translated by Geoff Bennington and Brian Massumi. Manchester, Manchester University Press.

MacDonald, M., 1997a, *'Doing ethnography in prisons: Italian initiatives on drugs, HIV/AIDS – initial identification of issues'*, Liverpool Health Authority, 1997, Health Prisons. Liverpool, Liverpool University Press.

MacDonald, M., 1997b, *Mandatory Drug Testing in Prisons*. Birmingham, CRQ and School of Sociology. ISBN 1859201112

Marcuse, H., 1964, *One-Dimensional Man: Studies in the ideology of advanced industrial society*. London, Ark.

Marshall, A., 1994, 'Sensuous sapphires: a study of the social construction of black female sexuality', in Maynard, M. and Purvis, J. (Eds.) 1994, *Researching Women's Lives from a Feminist Perspective*. London. Taylor & Francis, pp. 106–24.

Marx, K. and Engels, F., 1996, *The Communist Manifesto*. London, Phoenix.

Marx, K., [1887] 1977, *Capital*. London, Lawrence and Wishart.

Matoesian, G.M., 1993, *Reproducing Rape: Domination through talk in the courtroom*. Cambridge, Polity Press.

Mauthner, N. and Doucet, A., 1998, 'Reflections on a voice-centred relational method: analysing maternal and domestic voices' in Ribbens, J. and Edwards, R., (Eds.), 1998, *Feminist Dilemmas in Qualitative Research: Public knowledge and private lives*. London, Sage, pp. 119–46.

May, T., 1997, *Social Research: Issues, methods and process*. Buckingham, Open University Press.

Maynard, D.W., 1984, *Inside Plea Bargaining: The language of negotiation*. New York, Plenum.

Maynard, M. and Purvis, J. (Eds.) 1994, *Researching Women's Lives from a Feminist Perspective*. London. Taylor & Francis.

Merton, R.K., [1949] 1968, *Social Theory and Social Structure*. New York, Free Press.

Mills, C.W., 1973 [1959], *The Sociological Imagination*. Harmondsworth, Penguin.

Mills, C.W., 1956, *The Power Elite*. New York, Oxford University Press.

Morris, J., (1993) 'Gender and disability' in Swain, J. et al. *Disabling Barriers – Enabling Environments*. London, Sage.

Mumtaz, K. and Shaheed, F., 1987, *Women of Pakistan: Two steps forward, one step back?* London, Zed Books.

O'Donnell, M., 1993, 'Towards a sociology of the Capitalist World System', in O'Donnell, M. (Ed.), *New Introductory Reader in Sociology*, third edition, pp. 514–24 (Walton on Thames, Nelson).

Parsons, T. (1951) *The Social System*, New York, The Free Press [Ch 3]

Patrick, J., 1973, *A Glasgow Gang Observed*. London, Ayre Methuen.

Pawson, R., 1989, *A Measure for Measures: A manifesto for empircal sociology*. London, Routledge.

Piaget, J., 1971, *Structuralism*. London, Routledge and Kegan Paul.

Polsky, N., 1971. *Hustlers, Beats and Others*. Harmondsworth, Penguin.

Popper, K., 1980, *The Logic of Scientific Discovery*. London, Hutchinson.

Rock, P., 1979, *The Making of Symbolic Interactionism*. London, Macmillan.

Sawyer, H.G., 1961, 'The meaning of numbers' in Webb et al., 1996, *Unobtrusive Measures: Non-reactive research in the social sciences*. Chicago, Rand McNally.

Schlesinger, P., 1978, *Putting 'Reality' Together; BBC News*. London, Methuen.

Schlesinger, P., Murdock, G. and Elliott, P., 1993, *Televising Terrorism: Political Violence in Popular Culture*. London, Comedia.

Schutz, A., 1962, *The Problem of Social Reality*, The Hague, Nijhoff.

Scully, D., 1990, *Understanding Sexual Violence: A study of convicted rapists*. Boston, Mass., Unwin Hyman.

Sexwale, B.M.M., Violence against women: experiences of South African domestic workers', in Afshar, H. and Maynard, M., 1994, *The Dynamics of 'Race' and Gender: Some feminist interventions*. London, Taylor and Francis, pp. 196–221.

Simmel, G., 1908, *Soziologie. Untersuchungen über die Formen der Vegesellschaftung*. Berlin.

Standing, K., 1998, 'Writing the voices of the less powerful: reserach on lone mothers', in Ribbens, J. and Edwards, R., (Eds.), 1998, *Feminist Dilemmas in Qualitative Research: Public knowledge and private lives*. London, Sage, pp. 182–202.

Stringer, E.T., 1996, *Action Research: A handbook for practitioners*. Thousand Oaks, Calif., Sage.

Thompson, E.P., [1963] 1968., *The Making of the English Working Class*. (With revisions). Harmondsworth, Penguin.

Turok, B., 1987, *Africa: What Can Be Done?* London, Zed.

Waters, M., 1993, *Modern Sociological Theory*. London, Sage.

Weber, M., 1978, *Economy and Society*. Berkeley: University of California Press.

Weber, M., 1930, *The Protestant Ethic and the Spirit of Capitalism*. London, Allen & Unwin.

Weeks, J. and Holland, J., (Eds.) 1996, *Sexual Cultures: Communities, values and intimacy*. Basingstoke, Macmillan.

Westwood, S., 1984, *All Day Everyday: Factory and family in the making of women's lives*. London, Pluto.

Wheeler, E., 1994, 'Doing black mental health research: observation and experiences' in Afshar, H. and Maynard, M., (Eds.) 1994, *The Dynamics of 'Race' and Gender: Some feminist Interventions*. London, Taylor & Francis, pp. 41–62.

Whyte, W.F., [1943], 1955, *Street Corner Society: The social structure of an Italian slum*. (Enlarged edition). Chicago, University of Chicago Press.

Williams, M. and May, T., 1996, *Introductions to the Philosophy of Social Research*. London, UCL Press.

Williams, R., 1965, *The Long Revolution*. Harmondsworth, Penguin.

Williamson, J., 1978, *Decoding Advertisements*. London, Boyars.

Willis, P., 1977, *Learning to Labour*. Westmead, Saxon House.

Wright, W., 1975, *Six Guns and Society: A structural study of the Western*. Berkeley, University of California Press.

INDEX